Serving Our Country
And Paying The Price

To Ross:

Thank you for
Serving Our Country

Richard "Lambchops"

Price

To order additional copies, please contact us.
BookSurge, LLC
www.booksurge.com
1-866-308-6235
orders@booksurge.com

RICHARD "LAMBCHOPS" PRICE

SERVING OUR COUNTRY AND PAYING THE PRICE

2005

Serving Our Country
And Paying The Price

CONTENTS

The Story of the
Recon Platoon
"Echo" Company
2/502
101st Airborne Division

This book is dedicated to my Recon brothers:
Don "Wild Bill" Corey
Howard "Pappy" Grabill
Hector "Marty" Martinez
Gary "Four Eyes" Taylor

And the others who served in the platoon.

In memory of
James "Bull" Turnbull
And
Others that are no longer with us.

By: Richard Price

A Special Thanks To Barbara Ann Lane For All Her Work In The Final Editing Of This Book And For Her Patience While I Finished This Book.

PREFACE

S erving Our Country" is easy enough to explain. "And Paying The Price" is the difficult part. This latter portion of the title comes from the next to the last chapter "And Now, The Facts and Paying The Price". The majority of people have no concept of what the combat veteran went through or the permanent effects it has on the vet. Hopefully, this will help you understand some things and place a better perspective on the 'Nam vet.

The "And Paying The Price" portion of the title references the personalities, characteristics, problems, and attitudes of Vietnam veterans that spent time in combat units or in the jungle. Even though this book is about my specific unit, many of the stories and situations fit scenarios that could have described many other units.

I have heard many different figures, but somewhere between 11% to 15% of all Vietnam veterans were the actual combat troops and the balance were support units. The "And Paying The Price" portion of the book is primarily devoted to the "grunts" and "jarheads" that were in the jungle and experienced the hells of war.

The speculation portion is based upon bits and pieces of information gathered over the years that seem to add up. After I had completed the first revision of this book, I found the facts and also added a very personal chapter detailing the long-term effects of being in a war.

I hope this book will influence people's opinions and their attitudes in looking at the 'Nam vet with more understanding and in a favorable light.

THE REASON

The reason I wrote this book is so people can attempt to understand "us". In this specific context of "us" I am referring to the RECON platoon of "Echo" company of the 2/502. Although this book is about the Recon platoon and particular events, I am also referring to any 'Nam vet that is a combat vet and has seen the hells of war. I mention specific places such as Co Pung Mountain. But you could substitute another mountain name or elevation number; change a few words and this description fits much of what 'Nam vets saw and experienced. While I refer to "us" in this book, the context is for all of the combat vets, regardless of the branch of service.

If you are a parent, spouse, friend, child or grandchild of a combat veteran, I hope this will give you some understanding or insight to the problems that we carry and the demons that drove us there. The goal of this book is <u>not</u> for you to fully understand our problems. It is to give you enough insight or understanding to allow us room and to help us cope or deal with the situation. To fully understand the problems, you would have to experience them, and thank GOD you don't. This book will not contain obscenities, for I want my grandchildren (when I have them) or my friends' grandchildren to be able to read this at a young age. Or for any combat veteran of today, that their child, grandchild, parent, or relative can read this book and not be concerned with obscenities.

This book will not delve into the political side of Vietnam. Right, wrong, or indifferent, it is behind us and I believe there are enough books on the political portion of 'Nam. Besides, none of them make complete sense.

I am going to try and explain the different aspects or categories of things that we had to deal with. I will attempt to explain items separately and categorize them. It is up to you to visualize and realize that I am only explaining a singular aspect and many times all these facets are swirled into a chaotic frenzy. We referred to it as firefights, or combat assaults, or commonly, WAR!

The majority of this book is primarily written similar to a recipe. The ingredients are listed separately, as well as their function, and then you mix them all together to come up with a completed dish or meal. The ingredients are listed here to explain what molded us into what we were and also what we are today. This book will not flow like a novel or a mystery because this is not a novel or mystery. This is a book about the ingredients that we endured. The end of the book is more like a self-analyzing diary as I explain the end results and reflections of how it has affected my life.

I am going to attempt to use different everyday scenarios or experiences in an effort to place you in a state of mind so you can visualize some of what we went through. Obviously, the experience or effects won't be the same, but the idea is to help you feel or have some understanding of portions of what we saw. Some of the scenarios will be expanded beyond what would normally happen in everyday life, but it is an attempt to help state the experience.

You have to remember as you read this that I am not a writer or a manipulator of the English language. I am just attempting to tell you my story as I remember the events of 1970 and 1971.

Another reason for this book is the history it contains for our children and grandchildren. There have been many books on Vietnam, and friends have told me "it mentioned us" or "was about us" and none of them did or were. Well, this book is about US!

Hopefully, someday our children or grandchildren will read this book and understand why their father or grandfather just wants to be left alone. Or; someday when our children have children and one of them asks, "why are there times, when I look into your father's eyes, it appears that he is an empty shell?" Our children will be able to reply with some understanding and let them read this book to comprehend that we are an empty shell of what we used to be. Or; maybe while taking one of our grandchildren for a walk, our eyes are flittering back and forth, looking into the trees or bushes and noticing every little out-of-sync movement, and they don't understand why. Possibly one of them (the grandchild) is telling us a story and we have to keep asking them to repeat what was said or to speak up because our ears still ring from the combat assaults and other effects of war. Or; if we are taking them out to eat and we have to sit facing the door so we can see everyone and we act a little different than most grandparents do. Maybe they will ask why we sleep with a loaded handgun near us, and our children can possibly give some reasonable answer to explain why. Possibly, they will now be able to understand why we do not like being in malls or crowds. Maybe this will help. I hope that this can also help others to understand why combat veterans act or don't act the way people think we should.

To try and put on paper a perspective of the environment we encountered and survived, plus the complicated task of trying to define and explain the mental stress that we went through, as L.R.R.P.'s (pronounced lurps), is not an easy task. First of all, the words to explain the reality of 'Nam are not easily put onto paper. Words are only part of the story. The visual aspects, noises and smells tell another part of the story. And second, because I am just a storyteller. So bear with me as the story begins.

To start with, L.R.R.P. is an acronym for long-range reconnaissance patrol (or platoon). The Recon platoon during my tenure was called L.R.R.P.'s, Recondo's, as well as Recon. I must also point out that I am referring to "Echo" company or "E" company for the Recon platoon of the 2/502. I have found information on the Recon platoon of HHC or Headquarters of Headquarters Company. This was the original designation for the Recon platoon, but somewhere in late 1968 or early 1969 the Recon platoon switched to "Echo" or "E" company, and information on Recon started disappearing.

Recon men were also considered expendable. That meant if they went out and didn't come back, that was ok. If you wanted troops sent in to an area you weren't sure about, send in the L.R.R.P.'s. So much for being irreplaceable!

It is not easy to find a starting point in writing this because it has always been difficult to talk about being in the Recon platoon. I have always shunned away from talking about it. In previous conversations with other vets I felt out of place because I often thought we were in a different conflict. No one believed me when I mentioned we were in the field for weeks or months at a time. It was not until I came across some of the people mentioned in this book that I felt comfortable discussing the Recon platoon. I knew somebody believed me because they were there also. But that didn't happen until 28 years after I left 'Nam!

It should be stated up front that I am not trying to glorify what or who we were, or to put down or redefine other groups or books. I read a book called "RECONDO" which is an excellent book. Unfortunately, it was so good that I didn't sleep very well for the next few nights. The veteran that wrote the book was in a very dangerous and difficult situation. My "boonie" cap goes off to him and his unit.

This is not an attempt to say we were better or had a more dangerous assignment than other units; just different. But I have to interject that I don't know of anyone who had a more difficult assignment. I used to think that chopper pilots and door gunners had the worst job. I discarded that thought during the monsoons when we were soaked to the bone, colder than cold, and had been in the bush for several weeks. Helicopter crews went back to the base camp nightly and had a cold brew, hot shower, and a warm bed. We couldn't have made it without them, and I still have the highest respect for them, but they did go to the rear every day. To date, I have yet to talk to another vet who spent more concentrated time in the field or time in the bush verses time in the rear.

I should also make a clarification here because I refer to R.E.M.F's in several places in this book. R.E.M.F. stands for rear echelon mother f***er.

There were a lot of good people in the rear areas. We needed them, the supply Sergeants, company clerks, the communications people, truck drivers, cooks, and the list goes on and on. These people, when asked, will tell you they were in 'Nam and maybe had an occasional experience with a rocket attack, snipers, sappers, or incoming mortar rounds, but, otherwise will tell you honestly they had it relatively easy compared to the grunts. We needed these people to support us and they deserve our thanks.

A R.E.M.F. will tell you how many times he got drunk, or tell war stories with a smile on his face and a twinkle in his eyes, yet he probably never left the main compound except for an R&R! He was probably just an egotistical, homesick, or spoiled individual that complained about everything, regardless of how easy he had it. The war stories being told involved someone else or are contrived stories to fill a void in his life because he wasn't a combat soldier and his real combat experience was when he stubbed his toe running from a mouse that got into his footlocker! These people, we didn't need and still don't need; they deserve being mentioned only because they serve as a reminder of what I never wanted to be!

As the storyteller, I need to make you understand my position or function in the Recon platoon. The majority of the time I was the R.T.O. or radioman. For a short time in the end, I was the Platoon Sergeant, Platoon Leader, and a Team Leader. In the end, it was a matter of who carried the most rank in the unit.

In a small unit I had multiple functions; the same as everyone else. I maintained communications with the Battalion TOC (tactical operations center) and with the teams as they patrolled. I typically did not do the daily patrols, but one other person and I would stay behind with the rucks, guarding the equipment and maintaining communications. I also made sure we had clothes on our backs and enough food and other supplies. As time progressed and we had a lesser-experienced Lt., I tried to keep him in line, as did several others. Obviously, my point of view may be different because of my vantage point or disadvantage point. It is somewhat like witnessing a traffic accident where there are two witnesses on different corners. We saw the same accident from different angles, so our stories are different.

There are probably scores of other stories long forgotten in my memory bank, but this book's purpose is to help you understand "us" and not fill pages and pages with war stories. I will try to highlight some events that rate as a "10" on our stress level and a few events that help define some daily experiences. Some will be exciting, some boring, but our life in the bush was that way. Extreme highs and shifts in levels of emotions eventually helped to develop our state of being "hardcore".

There are places, throughout different chapters, where certain comments seem redundant. Often times I referenced specific comments or expressions because I felt it important to re-emphasize the influence or effect they had on us.

Ultimately, in the final analysis, this book was written to help people understand or comprehend the problems of combat veterans. After I wrote this book and edited it, I finally realized how much Vietnam had affected me. I have reread it numerous times in preparing it for publication. The more I have read the details, the more I comprehend the effects. Now that I comprehend the effects Vietnam had on me, I am able to cope with and enjoy my life better than I ever have. In order to cope with the problems from being in a war, I must simply stay within my boundaries. I know this will help those that I dedicated this book to. War is war, regardless of when it was. The end results are the same. Young men are wounded, young men die. Parents and families grieve over the loss, regardless if they were on the winning side. These facts are absolute and indisputable through time. Soldiers of the American Revolution had the same type of problems to contend with. People of today's conflicts will have problems similar to those that we have.

This book was not written with the intent to make money from the sales or to gain recognition by having a book in print. Originally, I did not intend to publish this book. Writing this book helped me, now I can only hope and pray it will help someone that has read this book. If this helps only one combat veteran with his problems, then it was worth all the work in preparing this book for publication. Hopefully, this book will help every reader in some way.

WHERE IT BEGAN

I was the usual draftee; Basic Training, Advanced Individual Training (A.I.T.), then Non Commissioned Officers (N.C.O.) School. The jump from Basic Training was the usual. I was a no frills private E-1. We all knew that eventually we would end up in Vietnam. In Advanced Individual Training, I was in 11Bravo or infantry training; otherwise it was the same, except in the end I signed up for Non Commissioned Officers School with a few other people. The difference is that we signed up for an 11F (Foxtrot) M.O.S. (Military Occupational Specialty) instead of the infantry 11B (Bravo). I believe this is where our destiny with the Recon platoon begins. I say "our" because, during Advanced Individual Training, I met a friendly individual by the name of Howard Grabill. He was considered an older guy by most of us, being he was probably four or five years older than the majority of us. We knew each other in passing and had a couple of conversations with each other. We were not the best of friends or anything, just casual acquaintances. In the military, people are always placed in alphabetical order, so Howie and I were in different barracks. Howie always outranked me because of alphabetical order; his name was ahead of mine but we were the same pay grade.

I contend our destiny for the Recon platoon started here because of future coincidences. The Recon platoon was made up primarily of handpicked individuals, whose profiles matched specific criteria, defined by some military brass believing that certain traits equated to Recon material. I mentioned "profiled" here, and while many people do not correlate it to the actual meaning, we all took a battery of tests in the beginning to determine what we would be best suited for. Whether it was a cook, truck driver, medic or infantryman, we were all "profiled" to determine our future in the military. Apparently Howie's profile and mine matched a particular niche the Army was looking for. That was probably the reason we were chosen for Non Commissioned Officers School; to give us more training, and to see if we would still fit the requirements after the additional schooling.

As coincidence had it, both Howie and I signed up for the "shake-n-bake" school, as it was known, for the 11F (Foxtrot) class. In military jargon, 11F was operations and intelligence, meaning that, in the rear areas, you were in intelligence (G-2 or S-2). In the field you would be a grunt of some form. Oddly enough, many people in Advanced Individual Training signed up for N.C.O.

School as 11Bravo or infantry. At the last minute several of us changed our applications to 11Foxtrot and we were the only ones accepted. It is amazing how a last minute change of mind will redefine your future and define the rest of your life.

The reason I signed up for N.C.O. School was to extend my time in the States. I had heard too many stories of soldiers returning from Vietnam with six or seven months left and ending up with assignments that were less than desirable, or having to extend their time in 'Nam to keep from having stateside duty. Neither of these situations appealed to me.

After N.C.O. School, my thinking proved correct. My On the Job Training (O.J.T.) was to place troops that had returned from 'Nam in temporary assignments, which were typically meaningless and a hassle.

I also wanted to go to Vietnam with more rank than I had. I figured my chances of being in a better position would improve with rank. I also knew it would keep me from pulling KP (kitchen police). KP is in essence a food server, dishwasher, and garbage handler-, none of which were on my list of favorite things.

Now in N.C.O. School, Howie and I were in the same situation as A.I.T. We still knew each other, but were in different barracks. I believe we occasionally hung around together, but after more than 30 years it's difficult to remember "casual" details. Being as N.C.O. School had a lot of class work, I am sure we had occasions to sit next to one another during classes.

Another interesting detail of going to N.C.O. School is advancement in rank. Basic Training through A.I.T. I was a Private E-1 as was Howie (I assume). We had 2 weeks of leave before reporting to Fort Benning as N.C.O. cadets or candidates with the rank of E-4 (skipped right past E-3!), so fortunately rank came very quickly. I was a Private E-1 for about 12 weeks; an E-2 for 2 weeks; an E-4 for 12 weeks; then became a Sergeant E-5 after that.

After 12 weeks of N.C.O. School we had 12 weeks of On the Job Training (O.J.T.). My On the Job Training consisted of personnel placement at Fort Benning, which had nothing to do with intelligence, only operations. I don't remember where Howie ended up but I believe it was in Texas.

As this book progresses note some coincidences occurring with Howie that begins to make one wonder.

IN COUNTRY

I went to Vietnam on September 8, 1970 and was assigned to the Headquarters Company, 2/22 of the 25th Infantry Division; also known as the "triple deuce". It was a mechanized unit, which traveled in APC's (armored personnel carriers) that were noisier than one can imagine. They were, in essence, a troop hauler that was built like a tank but without a turret and cannon, and shaped like a box. I had a couple of weeks in the rear and then went to the bush to work in the battalion tactical operations center (TOC) on second shift. I rarely mention much about the days in the 25th infantry because it was a brief experience and had little bearing on my tour of Vietnam. I received field experience there, but it was nothing like the Recon platoon. No ruck to hump or water to worry about. Hot food was provided for every meal and one of the biggest concerns was being stung by scorpions. Our mission there was known as the "Rome Plow" operation. We provided cover for the large bulldozers that were plowing down the jungle. I don't remember much of the make up of the Division except the 2/22. I am not even positive if the Division was completely mechanized or not.

The author shortly after his arrival in country.

Howie arrived in the country a few days later, I believe, but in a different unit in the South. We were totally unaware of the fact that the other was even in country. The first week of November I was transferred to the 101st Airborne Division. The unit of the 25th Infantry Division I was in, was being sent home. Being as I was still relatively new to the country, I was transferred north to "I" Corp, home of the "Screaming Eagles".

The 101st area of operation was basically the northwestern portion of "I" Corp, which is the northern portion of South Vietnam. Its area included the border to the Demilitarized Zone (DMZ) and west to Laos. Its terrain to the west, which we normally operated in, is mountainous and rugged.

Upon my arrival in Echo Company, I was informed I was to be in the Recon platoon and was given some camouflaged jungle fatigues (unlike others I had seen in the past, or anytime after), an M-16, supplies and a rucksack. As I was busy trying to figure out how best to fit the large pile of ammunition, food, grenades, canteens, personal items, and many other supplies in my newly acquired rucksack, another new arrival to Echo Company walked in the door to prepare his journey to the field. Any guesses at this point as to who the new arrival was? If you guessed Howie, you are correct! How coincidental. We were told that this was the number 1 rated platoon in the 101st but I didn't realize how right they were. Later we found out that the "O'Deuce" Recon platoon was rated number 1 for two years running. Considering approximately 4,000 men made up all the units in the 101st, that is quite a feat for about 20 to 25 men to hold. I have no idea what the considerations were in rating a platoon.

It makes one start to wonder. Advanced Individual Training and Non Commissioned Officers School together. We were in different parts of the U.S.A for our On the Job Training (O.J.T.), arrived in 'Nam in different units in the South, on different days, and BINGO! We arrived to go into the Recon platoon within a few hours of each other, in the north, on the same day. I believe a pattern or plan is starting to unfold here.

I believe that Howie and I were the only two from our N.C.O. class to go into a Recon unit, but I cannot be 100% positive of that. I did review the units that our classmates went into. Unfortunately, the descriptions gave very little information so it was very difficult to tell for sure.

Obviously we had no idea of what was ahead of us. What we didn't know was the Recon platoon was a very, very elite unit consisting primarily of handpicked individuals. An elite unit is one that is composed of the best men available. At the time, we were not told that the Recon platoon was an elite unit nor were we ever told that it was a special unit. While we suspected we were special, I did not find out for certain until almost 28 years later. So being in the Recon platoon was a privilege and an honor. It was also a very high-risk unit. It was said that the odds of making it back were less than favorable.

My first ride in a slick was coming up. I don't remember if it was that evening or the next day, but the time is irrelevant. We made our way to the chopper pad for our first lift, and I was learning to carry that awful thing on my back, called a ruck. My first ride in a slick was absolutely terrifying. If you could find that particular helicopter you would find my fingerprints deeply engraved on the steel post separating the door gunner from myself. I was sitting on the floor of the slick, not knowing what to expect from this event. One forgets things like; hundreds of soldiers do this daily, and centrifugal force will keep you from falling out as the helicopter banks. I had to bite my tongue so I wouldn't yell for help or anything else to embarrass myself, lest I let people know that this was my first ride on a slick. I had to remember that the vibrations I felt were normal and this thing actually would stay in the air. But you find it difficult to remember these theories as you are trying to breathe, or wondering if your sphincter muscles will ever relax enough to allow you to have a bowel movement before you turn 30. To say I was scared on my first ride is an understatement. It felt absolutely wonderful to have both feet on the ground again. As time progressed, these events became routine and much more tolerable. After having a few combat assaults (more on this term later) under my belt, that ride was a walk in the park.

As the helicopter sat down in the landing zone (L.Z.) Howie and I departed, and met up with the other members of the Recon platoon. We were on a landing zone with a Line Company (Delta), and I remember the Lieutenant (Lt.) wanted to depart as quickly as possible even though it was late in the day. To my knowledge, that is the only time I can remember being on a landing zone with someone else already there. Lt. Bridges had us move off the ridgeline and away from the Line Company. At that time I was wondering to myself, what was wrong with this guy? I thought there was safety in numbers. Why would Lt. Bridges and his band of 20 or so men want to go off on their own and depart from the "safety in numbers" theory? There must have been at least 100 soldiers in the Line Company. I wasn't sure of what I had gotten into, but I sure hoped this Lieutenant knew what he was doing and had his "stuff" in order.

As the evening progressed we found a suitable place to set up for the night. Once we stopped I was briefed by Platoon Sergeant Wakefield and instructed on how we were expected to carry a loaded M-16 (carried with a round in the chamber). After that, most of the time was spent with a guy named "Water Buffalo". Harry Hardin was making sure I was being taught the dos and don'ts of the Recon platoon, because if I screwed up it could be the end for him and all of us as well. There were tips on how to pack your ruck, how to whisper and not talk, how to set up for sleeping, how to eat quietly and many other things. Sort of like a big brother arrangement or a mini training session. It was then that I started to realize this little group might not be so bad. As I looked around I noticed everyone really seemed to have their "stuff" together. No talking or screwing off, only whispering and quiet movements. I was amazed that I couldn't hear any noticeable noise coming out of the Recon platoon's position but I could hear the Line Company that was still on the landing zone a few hundred meters away! I was accustomed to the noisy armored personnel carriers of the South and there were always screw offs or people who didn't fit in or get along with others. Here it was different. Everyone else's success or survival depended on the other person as well. Teamwork or reliability of the other person was of the utmost importance here.

Now I was starting to understand what the Recon platoon was about. Late that night, I really understood why Lt. Bridges wanted to move away from the Line Company. I can remember sitting up: I think I was pulling my turn on guard or possibly just couldn't sleep. I could hear the noise from the Line Company. It sounded like a small party going on. I could hear music and laughing going on! A short time later there was an explosion and some gunfire.

Apparently, a sapper threw a satchel charge into the machinegun nest, killing 2 American soldiers and wounding another thirteen. A sapper was a North Vietnamese Army soldier (N.V.A.) who was taught how to crawl through places one would think impossible to go through and typically carried an explosive device and a handgun. A sapper normally spent years learning how to crawl and was very difficult to detect and stop. Now I was really starting to believe this thought process of "quiet was better".

The following morning we had moved out from our night defensive position (later referred to as a NDP) and were following a trail when two North Vietnamese appeared off to our right. I think they were more surprised than we were because they didn't hear us. We exchanged a few brief moments of gunfire, retrieved a barrel for an M-60 machinegun and we had one less member of the North Vietnamese Army to contend with. We believed the barrel had been taken the night before from the Line Company. This concept of being in a small group and being quiet was starting to look very promising!

After the brief exchange we thought "Water Buffalo" might have been hit but soon realized it was my hot brass that had given us the impression that he had been wounded. During the exchange of gunfire I was unaware that some of my hot brass (empty shell casings from my M-16) were going down "Water Buffalo's" back and he was receiving small burns from them. And if you are reading this Harry, my apologies and give me a call so we can reminisce.

Recon units are technically supposed to minimize contact and search an area for enemy activity, report it to higher ups and call in support. That is, if we were in range of support. Support being artillery, mortars, air strikes or gunships. This was what we typically tried to do. It was like a big game of hide-and-seek, lasting for weeks on end in some of the ugliest environment, with guns and bullets that were very real. Here we were the hunter and the hunted; and in our case, we were considered a trophy.

As time progressed I had a deep appreciation for Lt. Bridges, as did everyone else. If I remember correctly he later became the Commanding Officer for a Line Company. A short time into my adventure with the Recon platoon the radio operator (R.T.O.) was going home and Lt. Bridges informed me that I would be humping the radio. This was because I had radio experience in the South when I was with the 25th Infantry Division; another tip that this was not a normal unit. I was a buck Sergeant (E-5) and the platoon radioman (R.T.O.). I thought this was kind of odd. There were others with less rank and experience than me so why was I humping a PRC-77 radio that added an extra 20 or 25 lbs. to an already overweight ruck? Maybe I did have more experience with the radio than most of the others, but did that make a difference? But the more I thought about it, the more I realized that I had a pretty powerful accessory on my back that could come in handy some day, so I conceded that it wasn't so bad. Later on I realized how important the position of the radioman (R.T.O.) was.

The rank in the Recon platoon was also a give away to the fact that we were different. Most Line Companies had Platoon Sergeants and Team Leaders that were Sergeants, but the balance was made up of Spec. 4's (Specialist 4th class) or P.F.C.'s (Private First Class; E-3). The Recon platoon had more Sergeants than all the other ranks in the platoon combined. The Recon platoon also probably had more Sergeants than the normal Line Company. My assumption for this, in looking back, was because of the possibility of high casualties; a large majority of the Recon men could have led the unit if the situation required it. As a comparison, the Recon platoon had similar organization to Special Forces units.

It should also be pointed out that normally we did not wear any indication of rank or unit in the bush. Some of the uniforms had the 101st Airborne insignia (regular and subdued) on them but that was it. We did not even wear the pin-on type of rank. That also included the Lieutenant.

THE RUCKSACK AND THE HUMP

Being as the rucksack carried all of our basic needs, this is probably an appropriate place to explain about the "ruck" and "the hump". As I mentioned in the beginning, one of the purposes of this book is to try and shed light on the environment and mental condition of L.R.R.P.'s or Recon men. Let me start by defining an overweight ruck.

Envision, spreading out on your living room floor the food you consume in a day (all the food including snacks and fluids). Multiply it by 9 to 12 times, for a start. But that's just the food. True enough we were able to obtain all the L.R.R.P. rations we wanted, which were freeze-dried meals. Most of the rations were quite good, especially the beef and rice, which was my favorite. Chicken stew, spaghetti, chicken & rice, beef stew, and scalloped potatoes were all good. Chili con carne wasn't so good and there was another version but I can't remember the name. Anyway, we typically carried enough freeze-dried food for no less than 6 to 8 days, and "C" rations to fill in the balance. Everyone carried different combinations and quantities of food. We always traded for our favorites. I remember "Water Buffalo" loved the scrambled eggs in the "C" rations. He would trade almost anything for them. The "C" rations had fruits that were also good. The peaches mixed with a canned pound cake were always a favorite combination.

We were supposed to be resupplied every 5 days with food and other necessities but monsoons and fog always hampered our resupply. We always tried to carry enough food for approximately 10 to 12 days or more. Now remember, that's just food. Add 1000 rounds of ammo for the M-16 for which I carried 30 magazines and the balance in bandoleers in the ruck. Water-depends upon the time of year. In the monsoons 5 or 6 quarts were all that was needed but during the hot times I would carry a 5 quart on top of the radio; 2 quarts on the pistol belt and another 3 quarts on the side or in the ruck.

As I have hinted through this writing about being a special unit, the food was also another hint. We didn't know that other units did not have the luxury of receiving all the freeze-dried food or heating tabs to cook with or warm up with. We always got whatever we asked for, or needed, but being as we were isolated from other units we never knew that we were receiving preferential treatment.

So we have covered beans, bullets, and water. Now all we have left is hand grenades, smoke grenades, claymore mines, radio, spare battery, an ammo box with camera, paper, envelopes, etc., hot chocolate or coffee, heating tabs to cook with (remember- no fires!), cream, sugar, salt, pepper, toilet paper, poncho and poncho liner to sleep in (or under), a few cans of soda or beer (drank warm), tooth paste, tooth brush, shaving gear, C-4 explosives (for extra bang and in case we ran out of heating tabs), a long antennae and a few other things I probably missed.

Fully loaded ruck: quite possibly the author's because of radio and fixed bayonet.

Because of the noise factor, shovels, helmets, air mattresses and many other things were not included in our inventory. We were concerned with carrying the vitals: ammo, explosives, and food, and plenty of all.

I don't remember having my ruck weighed but a couple of my old friends do and Don "Wild Bill" Corey said his was somewhere between 100 and 120 pounds. He believed the lightest was 85-pounds. This also helps to explain our state of mentality; remember that we were struggling up or down a mountain, in the monsoons, with a heavy ruck. We were also in a constant mode for a firefight. Because we never knew when contact would happen, we were always walking with our thumb on the safety and ready to go to " rock & roll" (full automatic). And yes, we always carried a round in the chamber. Struggling may be a mild word to explain traversing with the ruck. It was, at times, the hardest thing to handle because of the slipping, sliding, and trying to be aware of everything going on around you. Plus it was just plain heavy and hard on the body! And we had to maintain silence.

Now as you are trying to envision this monster of a load on your back you also have to remember that we had to get from the ground to the upright position. This was not an easy thing to accomplish. Most of the time it was easiest to have the ruck loaded and on the ground. Then sit on the ground in front of it and strap it on. Then rolled on all fours like a dog and eventually stand up. The other option was to grab a strap with both hands, swing it over one shoulder and work the other arm through the strap. The latter version was sometimes easier if it was muddy or slick, but if one didn't swing it right the landing could be uncomfortable and somewhat painful. It was also common to carry a towel (olive drab green) to use as extra padding so the straps would not cut into our shoulders so badly. We had to do this silently. Nothing like the weightlifters you see on television that give a loud grunt or yell as they lift. As these events were occurring we had an M-16 next to us, knowing that we were vulnerable during this time and always had to be ready for the enemy

A reasonable thought for you to make physical comparisons to carrying a ruck is; the next time you are lugging a 40-pound bag of salt down the basement steps to put in the water softener, remember that we were carrying the equivalent of 2 ½ to 3 bags up or down mountains in the mud and we did not have steps or handrails to help.

It is true that the ruck did get lighter day by day. We often would eat more of the "C" rations the first couple of days because they were heavier. The extra battery was put in the radio and the old one destroyed at some point. This was done by twisting the wires together so it would eventually burn up, otherwise it could be used on a booby trap against us. This would reduce the weight some. We needed to maintain our water supply, grenades, and ammunition, and with the radio the weight stayed constant. Yes, it did lighten some as the days went on but it still tipped the scales at a hefty weight.

Howard "Pappy" Grabill's ruck, weapon, and vest with 40m.m. grenades.

One of the keys to relating to the physical problems of humping the ruck, is the "humpers" (us). While it is true that we were young and tough, the average Recon man was typically between 5'7" to 6'1" and weighed 145 pounds to 175 pounds. Some were taller ("Smitty", for example was probably 6'4"), some weighed more, but considering body weight verses ruck weight; we carried a lot of weight.

Try to envision sitting with your feet hanging out of a helicopter door as the cobras are firing away and you are preparing to land and secure the landing zone (L.Z.). You are doing this with a 100 to 120 pound ruck on your back. It complicates matters tremendously because moving quickly with a ruck on your back is difficult, to say the least.

Distance. Standing with a heavy ruck is one thing, walking is another. Fortunately, Recon teams were not intended to travel great distances most of the time. But we had an occasion or two that involved more than a typical day's hump. A typical day if there was such a thing may only cover 500 or 1000 meters to maybe 1500 meters.

I can remember an occasion one day, after a re-supply, that involved traversing approximately eight miles to a firebase (for reasons that I cannot remember). There are approximately 1600 meters or 1.6 clicks (1.6k) to a mile. Eight miles is over 12.5k in one day! And all the time we were lugging the ruck!

As I discuss distance you must also consider that I am referring to map distance not actual distance covered. On a map we may travel 1,000 meters, which is somewhat "as the crow flies" distance. In the mountains it may be 2 or 3 times the distance because we may have had to go around the mountain or follow a ridgeline around because of it being too steep. We may have had to break trail as we went or traverse downed trees. This doesn't even consider the worst factor of all, the monsoons.

During the 'soons (monsoons) it was not uncommon to take 4 steps forward and slide back 3 because it was so muddy. It was a very slow process for going up a mountain. Also consider that we were wet, cold, tired, ready for a firefight, and hungry.

Side effects of the heavy ruck were leg cramps, sore shoulders and back problems. To describe the pain of a Charlie horse in the leg muscles is hard to do. I often thought someone had beaten me in the back of the legs with a ball bat because they hurt so much. At night during the 'soons I would be wet all day and the last thing I wanted was to get wet from going out to relieve myself when I had finally gotten reasonably dry and somewhat warm. I would get on my knees and lean out from the side of my hooch made from ponchos and relieve myself. About half an empty bladder later the leg cramps would announce their arrival and, gritting my teeth in pain, I would continue to relieve myself while making an effort to stay dry; an experience and feeling I can't forget.

After a long hump, nothing felt better than to unstrap the ruck and rest my back and legs before setting up for the night or eating. Sometimes we were so tired from the hump that we would drag some "C" rations out of the ruck and eat them cold. At this point I am lost for words that could describe the tired and achy feeling of the body, the soreness of the back and shoulders, and the feeling of the legs after the hump. And I am not even discussing the condition of being mentally tired or emotionally drained at this point. There will be more on those portions later.

Once one mastered balancing the ruck and learning how to walk with it, it was amazing how agile we could be. I don't remember ever seeing anyone falling down because of their ruck, but after over 30 plus years, details of this nature could have easily been forgotten. Oddly enough we became so accustomed to walking with the balanced load that, with the ruck off, sometimes normal walking seemed awkward. One of my problems after I left the field was tripping and stumbling while going up steps. I can remember occasions walking down wet logs during the monsoons without problems. I don't know if it was the shift in my center of gravity or the added weight that gave more traction, but I walked places with the ruck that I didn't think was possible.

Humping up the side of a steep mountain with a full ruck.

If you are thinking to yourself that your back hurts from reading this then I am describing it well because it did cause aching backs and back problems. Jumping ahead 30 years, 3 of the 5 of us that have reunited after 'Nam have dead spots in their backs from carrying the rucks and all of us have back and knee problems. I also found out that some of the men did fall face forward when carrying the ruck.

When mentioning the load of our rucks I noted that, other than a few people carrying extra socks, we did not carry extra clothes. Typically in the monsoons you were wet all the time so dry socks didn't mean much. Being we received clean clothes every other resupply or about every 10 to 12 days, the pants or shirt might not last as long or stay intact the whole time. It was not uncommon to be sitting across from a friend, after a day's hump was over, and attempting to warm the body with hot food, coffee, or hot chocolate and his private parts were dangling out of his pants. They may have ripped open that day or maybe a couple of days earlier. Modesty and hygiene were things that we forgot existed because at that point, they were irrelevant. And yes, after 10 to 12 days in the same clothes, we were quite grungy and foul smelling! But when we received clean clothes this didn't mean we were able to clean up. A shower a month was a real treat!

Hopefully by now you are starting to put together a mental picture of the physical difficulties we endured while humping the bush. The picture is very hard to describe because so much of what is written must be experienced to be fully understood. It is like a woman explaining childbirth to a man. We can understand but not fully comprehend the contractions and pain of delivery. I can only hope a reader can understand the words because comprehension is very difficult without experiencing it. I also hope and pray that those reading this never have to experience a situation similar to what I have described. Another drawback of being in the bush is, what do you do if you twist an ankle? Tie the bootlaces tighter and go on!

In writing about the ruck I have put in a few words about carrying the ruck. I have told about slipping and sliding, distance, and things of that nature but I did not actually describe humping. The ability to go up and down mountains with a ruck on is an art, not a science.

To start with it is appropriate to explain spacing in a hump. If you watch any war movie invariably it shows men walking close together, maybe talking, sometimes smiling or occasionally chuckling, some walking with a lit cigarette or walking side by side. And always, walking too close together! The Vietnam segment of the movie "Forrest Gump" is a good example of this. As we humped it was important to keep proper spacing. The point and slack men may have different spacing than the middle or rear guard, but it was very important to "keep your space".

The point and slack men were our early warning team. They led the way or broke trail when necessary. It was up to them to spot ambushes or booby traps. These men needed to be experienced and also good.

The rear guard often times walked backward part of the distance to see if we were being followed. Sometimes the rear guard would lag behind 25 to 100 meters to see if we were followed.

The purpose of spacing was because of ambushes and booby traps. If a booby trap was tripped or sprung, the number of wounded would be minimized. The closer we were together the more of us could be taken out by a booby trap or ambush.

The North Vietnamese and Viet Cong preferred to wound rather than kill. A wounded soldier required at least one or two other soldiers to help them. One wounded soldier took out three men while a dead soldier removed only one. The more we were spaced apart, the less wounded we could receive.

In movies you see troops at an arm's length from each other or almost on top of each other. If the trail were easy to traverse we would string out. Sometimes the middle spacing might be 30 or 40 feet between men. If the trail was slick as during the monsoons, we might have to be closer to help one another up. As I watch war movies, I almost laugh as I see them too close together and I try to yell at the TV screen to tell them to space out but it is to no avail. And if you notice, in the war movies showing troops bunched up, the casualties are high. I never walked point or slack because I carried the radio but I do remember walking rear guard with Hector "Marty" Martinez a few times in the monsoons. The last men through had a very difficult time on the trail because it had gotten muddier as everyone else had already slid or slipped on it. We would keep turning around and walk backwards for a few paces at a time to see if we were being followed or probed. Many times we thought we were being followed but never saw anyone, but the N.V.A. were excellent at keeping out of sight. Plus the noises of the jungle can play tricks on the mind.

As I said, humping is an art. Techniques are different on dry trails verses muddy trails. If the trail was dry we did not need to dig the side or heel of the boot in to make traction. When it was muddy we had to dig deeper and sometimes pause between steps to maintain the ground we had just gained or keep our balance. Going down hill can be just as tricky as going up. Because of the weight and mud, it was easiest to walk on the heels.

Once I learned the art of humping I found that walking with more weight on the back of my heels was easier. Being as the toes have to push up on every step, it was easier on the legs to be more flatfooted and balance the weight to the rear. It was also easier to balance on the heel of the foot compared to the toe because the heel doesn't give like toes do. Even today I walk that way but, because I'm not carrying a ruck, I bounce some as I walk.

Another thing on a hump that slowed us down were the "wait a minute" vines. These vines had small barbs on them and they seemed to know we were coming down the trail and would grab our uniforms. It was like they had some sort of intelligence.

When we awakened in the morning we ate, rolled up our ponchos (hooch), loaded the ruck, and saddled it on for another hump. But what happened if we had diarrhea from the water or our stomachs were churning from a 24-hour bug? We would slow down a little but go on. In the bush we did not have the option of calling in sick! Rain or shine, in sickness or health, we humped!

On the trail many other obstacles were often encountered. We might have to climb over a fallen tree. That in itself was not so bad but I never mentioned that not all of the uniforms were the right size! There were occasions when the pants were too big, or worse, too small. Going across trees is when we would most likely hear a "rip".

On the 8-mile hump mentioned earlier in the book, I had the pair of pants that were too small. Crossing a fallen tree started a rip. A couple of fallen trees later the rip involved the rear end. As the rip grew in length I needed some small rope to hold the pants together. By the end of the hump my pants (what was left of them) were at my ankles and I was basically wearing my jungle shirt and ruck!

Sometimes during the hump we would break for a short time and sometimes eat. Humping took a lot of energy out of you and longer humps required more breaks. I don't remember anyone in Recon carrying extra body weight. The hump worked off all the excess fat.

Humping could also be a slower process than you might think. If we were on a trail that appeared "hot" or had signs of enemy movement we would be more cautious and move at a slower rate of speed, and all the time, still carrying the ruck!

Some obstacles create other problems in the hump. We had followed an old road, if memory serves me right, I believe it was near an abandoned firebase. No big deal to this point, but there was a ravine that was too steep to traverse down and the bridge was a skeleton of I-beams. The I-beams were probably 12 to 18 inches wide. Too many years have passed for that detail to be clear, but regardless, it made it touchy to cross. One by one we crossed the bridge's I-beams until all had safely crossed. I believe we were about fifteen to twenty feet in the air at the deepest point of the ravine and if one fell more than 7 or 8 feet with a ruck the impact would probably finish him off! That was one of those cases where we held our breath, put our trust in our instincts and sense of balance, said a prayer or two and started the slow walk across!

This is most likely the bridge we humped across.

As we are discussing movement from place to place, this is a good place to interject where we didn't hump or go.

We didn't enter villages. We had one occasion when we were sent to a small compound near a town called Mai Loc close to the Demilitarized Zone (DMZ). We spent a couple days there at the most, building bunkers because we thought we were going to have some easy time. We were tricked into building them for someone else and then we were sent back to the bush. That was during our ninety plus consecutive day stint in the field. Other than that, I didn't enter any villages nor was I even close to any. Most vets will talk about being in such and such town, or seeing on TV places they recognize from being there or driving through them. I cannot place a single landmark or town because I wasn't in any!

RECON, SOME SHORT MEMORIES

L t. Bridges was a good leader from what I knew of him. I was his R.T.O. for a period of time. If he had his canteen out and I was thirsty, he would offer me a drink and vice versa. I admired his philosophy and sense of responsibility. He wouldn't ask anyone to do something that he would not do himself.

In our unit we had a secure radio device or Delta-1 which weighed approximately 25 pounds. This attachment, for lack of a better term, scrambled our transmissions, so only those with a matching unit that was also "punched" the same could unscramble and listen to our transmission. This allowed us to talk in the clear. Otherwise we would talk in the open using nicknames and codes, which we will get into later on. This device was passed from soldier to soldier on a regular basis to help share the load. Lt. Bridges always took his turn carrying the Delta-1 even though he was the ranking member. I think that set the tone for those in the Recon platoon because it showed that we were a team and everyone carried their weight regardless.

Carrying one's weight was another indicator that the Recon platoon was different. Anyone that did not fit in or had problems with cutting it in the platoon simply went back to the rear and was reassigned. That was very unusual because whether you liked it or not you had to hump the bush in a Line Company and it was difficult to change units. In Recon it was just a matter of saying "you're out" and away you went.

Time is a fleeting thing in the bush. Some things you cannot forget regardless of how hard you try. Other things blend together so well that it is impossible to remember details. In small units in the bush, as we were, we were constantly on guard, 24 hours a day, 7 days a week. Mentally, we could never let down to relax because we were always in the jungle. So time became a fleeting thing. Some people went, some came and all of a sudden you realize some newby in the bush is now your friend.

It was hard to remember Lt. Bridges leaving and Lt. Townsend arriving. I don't remember exactly when Gary Taylor arrived either but one day he was there and we were friends. I cannot remember all the details but suddenly we were shacking up together or "hooch mates". I assume we made this arrangement because I carried the radio and he was to call in artillery. Hooch mates are two people that keep their ponchos set up together so setting up at night is easier and quicker to do. A hooch was typically two ponchos tied together to create a shelter. In time you also know their habits and develop a bond and trust in that person. In as small a group as the Recon platoon, trust and dependability is a necessity, not an option. The friendships developed through the experiences we encountered will follow us to our graves because they are too deep to lose. "Four Eyes" eventually became Gary's nickname because he needed glasses. "Four Eyes" and I slept back to back for many months on end during the 'soons because that was the only way we were able to keep warm. We also set up together in the warmer periods so he could have access to my radio as well as help respond to the situation reports at night.

Gary "Four Eyes" Taylor and Richard "Lambchops" Price, the author.

As for me, I am "Lambchops". The name developed because as we were always in the bush, I rebelled against shaving (as did most of the others) and had mutton chop sideburns. Besides, who cared? No one ever saw us. We stayed in the jungle, rarely came out and when we did we were kept away from other soldiers. Apparently the Army didn't want our attitude showing to other troops. Or maybe by keeping us away from the grunts, they were hoping we would not realize how different we were.

We were like everyone else at Thanksgiving. A few days in the rear and back in the bush. Christmas was similar except for the Bob Hope show. It was also a hint we were different but we didn't realize it. It was a cease-fire and almost everyone was going to see the show. We were told we had "reserved" seats but we figured it was just a line of bull. When we arrived we told the M.P.'s that we were supposed to have reserved seats (as probably did everyone else). When they asked who we were and we told them we were the O'Deuce Recon platoon their response was "oh, you guys!" They pointed to an empty area just to the left of center stage in the front. They indicated it was saved for us. Even though there were no chairs they informed us that we were to have a seat on the ground, right in front of the stage. We sat in front of all the Generals and other brass. Behind us and to our right was Nuygen Kao Ky; Vice President of South Vietnam.

Picture of Bob Hope and Gloria Loring from our front row seat.

By the way, the show was great. There should be a shrine put up for

Bob Hope for all the shows he put on and all the time he spent away from his family. More should be said about all the great work he did and the morale he improved but that would probably be another book.

As we were sitting there watching this fantastic show I was thinking to myself. How did we get these seats? Who are we or what are we to have this privilege?

Another person to enter the picture just prior to Christmas is Hector Martinez. "Marty" as he became known, was and still is a Chicago area person. "Marty" was a couple of years older than most of us. I believe he was 23 or 24 at the time, a very old man in our unit. I was barely 21, Gary was 20, and Howie, because of his senior citizen status was nicknamed "Pappy". Howie was 25 or 26 if memory serves me right.

Another soldier to enter the picture at the first of the year was Don Corey. Don quickly progressed to be known as "Wild Bill", a nickname given to him by Jim Turnbull (also referred to as "Bull"). "Wild Bill" and I became friends and during our time together we were unbeatable in the card game of Spades. "Wild Bill" had to get into a fight just to get into the Recon platoon!

"Wild Bill" told me that a Staff Sergeant (E-6) associated with the Recon platoon but rarely in the field, had pulled rank on the First Sergeant (E-8) to get him in the Recon platoon. Something different had to be going on for this event to have happened. An E-6 doesn't outrank an E-8 and doesn't get away with a situation like that unless there are special ties or connections associated with the E-6 or the Recon platoon.

Another person to enter the picture during this time frame was Lt. Townsend. The Lt. had very little experience, if any, before coming to the Recon platoon. He was a tall guy from somewhere in the West. Montana or Wyoming if I remember correctly. His "care" packages he received from home included salamis or preserved meats of some sort in about one pound sticks. He never liked these so he passed them on to me. Lt. Townsend was not the most popular person in the Recon platoon. As he got more experience he became a little more accepted. His personality was ok but he didn't know much of what he was doing and that made things more difficult to contend with. "Bull", "Water Buffalo", and I tried to keep him in line.

Recon humping in water.

One of the things the Lt. did that never settled well with any of us, was walking through the streams. I don't know if he was born crawling in water but he loved to walk through it. I believe he thought that it made us more difficult to be tracked or followed. There were cases when this was important but water follows the lowest possible path on the ground. This is simple physics and basic gravity. We preferred the high ground, to be safer. In a low area you can be ambushed from many different angles, where on the high ground it is easier to be defensive, plus you have a better vantagepoint for observing.

In referring to streams it is appropriate to mention hygiene here. We all did the usual of brushing of our teeth daily, a few shaved on a regular basis but that was about the limit of hygiene. We went out to the bush on December 31, 1970 and it was <u>21</u> days before we attempted to wash off in a cold stream some of the excess crud we had accumulated. This attempt is similar to washing your hands, face and arms when you sit down to eat, and it was not a shower. And when I say attempted, that is about the limit of it. The water was very cold in the stream and it could be compared to taking a cold shower outside when the weather is between 50 and 60 degrees. So obviously, we didn't get very clean. Can you imagine going three months without showering? I can recall occasions when we had a couple of newbys arrive. As they were being introduced to us, they had to hold their noses and we could see them grimace from our odor. Walking in water daily or being in mud and wet all the time or just being smelly from perspiration during the summer made us blend into the environment. It was not unusual to go for weeks at a time before attempting to wipe off excess grung, and soap wasn't used because of the scent. Not only that, even when we did wash off, it would only last through the end of the day at the longest. Besides, what good would it do to wash daily? We were camouflaging ourselves in the bush by smelling like it.

I think it is important to mention a couple of the old timers at this point: Jim Turnbull or "Bull" and Harry Hardin or "Water Buffalo". I believe these two represented the experience and persona of a Recon man. Both were smart and well respected by all; a little crazy as well but that is beside the point. They were both experienced in the bush but were not arrogant about what they knew or how they acted. Both wanted to help or teach us about survival in the bush. You could sit and talk (whisper) with them and know you were in the presence of experience.

"Bull" and "Water Buffalo" were both there when I arrived and still in Recon when I left. Both were recovering from wounds received at Co Pung when I left the field.

"Bull" was not huge but was as sturdy as an oak tree. He was probably 6'2", maybe a tad more, with reddish hair. I didn't have the pleasure of spending a lot of time with "Bull", as he was one of the Team Leaders. When we split up, the Lt. and I traveled with the other team.

My guess is that we were probably in a platoon size unit about half the time. The number in the full platoon averaged about twenty people, maybe a couple more on some occasions and a couple less on others.

"Water Buffalo" looked bulky which is where he got his nickname, I believe. He really wasn't heavy but built like an ox and almost as strong.

As people enter Recon, like "Wild Bill", "Pappy", "Four Eyes", "Marty", others and myself, these two spent time with us to make sure we knew the hows and whys of Recon. They wanted to make sure that they did everything to improve our odds of survival, and wanted their experience to help us in some way. It also improved their chances for making it out in one piece. It was people like these two that reduced the chances of our names appearing on a monument many years later. I also firmly believe that if there were more "Bulls" and "Water Buffalos" in other units during the war, that more young men would have had better chances of survival and we would have fewer names on a wall in Washington D.C. A special thanks goes out to these two and others like them.

Unfortunately, we lost "Bull" in 1972. From what I have been told, after he returned home, he could not deal with what he had gone through. As I understand it, he had survived some situations where he was one of only a few survivors and carried survivors' guilt. May he rest in peace.

Like I mentioned earlier, several men came and several went. I am intentionally not listing all the names because I cannot remember when everyone came and went. I will list everyone I can remember where applicable in this book. No disrespect is intended.

Lt. Townsend was with us for a few months and Lt. Barnett replaced him later. Lt. Barnett was a much more likable person. He was with us through Co Pung (see the chapter for details) but I don't think he went back to the field with us. I heard he froze on Co Pung but I was on the other side of the mountain. I don't remember a lot of Lt. Barnett on Co Pung but there are a lot of things about that event that I cannot remember. I replaced Lt. Barnett for a short time as Platoon Leader after Co Pung.

An incident that is appropriate to place here is the story of an unexploded bomb. Being we did not carry a bathroom scale with us, I don't know if it was a 500-pounder or a 750 pounder. Regardless, it was awful big! We had come across it while moving from one night defensive position to another. I also believe we had a Vietnamese scout with us at that time. I was told that his eyes almost popped out of his head when he first saw it. Upon finding the bomb we moved back down the trail to a safer distance. As it was late in the day and being somewhat arrogant, I called in the find as a very large unexploded grenade. By our luck it also happened to be the time when we changed our radio frequencies and call signs.

Changing the Standard Operating Index (S.O.I.) was sometimes hectic because of mistakes in setting the correct frequencies on the radio, call signs or whatever. This was done on a regular (typically monthly) basis for security. All changes happened at midnight.

We also had a Battalion X.O. (Executive Officer), a Major who was second in command, and not particularly fond of Recon. He was referred to as the Kraut Bastard as he had German heritage.

When midnight came and went, there was a communications check to make sure all the changes went smoothly. When the battalion tactical operations center attempted to raise us on the new frequency and could not, the Executive Officer was awakened and informed of the situation. He was probably in a deep sleep (something we did not do) and was upset for being awakened. We were nearest the firebase Checkmate at that time so he had them fire "Willie Pete(r)" or "White power" artillery rounds (white phosphorus) toward us to wake us up. We were already awake trying to raise the battalion tactical operations center on the radio. Later we found out they were on the wrong frequency. Anyway, these rounds were air bursting above the 500-pound bomb we found earlier in the day. If any of the rounds had detonated the bomb, we would have all been history. I switched the radio back to the old frequency and was able to raise the firebase and had them "check fire" or cease firing. We never received an apology for that.

The next day we called in and had some time delay fuse and extra C-4 plastic explosive brought in. When it was time to blow it, I called in to have them clear the air space because a bomb that size could throw debris high enough to take out a passing helicopter. They asked me why they needed to clear the air space and when I explained the size of the bomb they finally understood our concerns. Another reason for not disclosing that the "grenade" was actually an unexploded bomb was the N.V.A. might have been aware of it. If they were, then they would know of our approximate position because we assumed they listened in to our transmissions. Also, if I had let it be known that we were sitting next to a 500-pound bomb, one well-placed mortar round near the bomb could have taken us all out!

The explosives were placed and the fuse was lit. If memory serves me correctly Kaufman was the one that placed the explosives and lit the fuse. I remember him removing his watch and other metallic objects before approaching the bomb. I believe a fifteen or twenty-minute fuse was placed on it. The bomb was in a valley and we were on top of the ridgeline but on the backside of it. We were probably 200 meters at the most from it when it went off. We thought we were far enough from it but we were wrong. Dirt was flying everywhere. Tree limbs and trees were flying over us. Anything that was in the area was now airborne. Fortunately, most of the larger pieces flew passed us but several of us had dirt in our eyes and I think one or two were hit by flying dirt clods.

When we left the area, we humped through where the bomb had been. It had cleared out everything! There wasn't a tree left standing in the area. It was amazing the power and energy of those things.

Since we are on the subject of bombs there is another incident I'll throw in here. Not quite as close a call as the last.

It was sometime during the hot days, exactly when, I'm not sure but we were taking a break during the midday heat. As usual, a card game was being played on the back of someone's ruck. I believe "Wild Bill" and I were winning at Spades. We had been informed the previous day that a "daisy cutter" or commando vault, as it was sometimes called, was going to be dropped on the other side of the ridgeline from us. We were better than two miles away and I think "danger close" was considered 1½ miles.

A daisy cutter is shaped like a top or wedge with a long detonator on it to create an airburst and weighs in at a hefty 10,000 pounds. One of the goals of this device is to clear out a landing zone for two or three helicopters plus remove any enemy in the area. These bombs are not precision-guided bombs like we hear about today. They were pushed out of the back of a cargo plane with a parachute attached and would drift to their destination.

We were informed early in the morning that the bomb drop had been canceled so we forgot about it. But, nobody called us to let us know the drop was back on. As we were playing cards, with a deck that had absorbed its share of moisture through the months, I dropped one, which was common because the cards were thick and warped. I happened to look up and saw a huge plume of smoke and fire. My first impression was, they had just dropped the Atom Bomb! A couple of seconds later it dawned on me that they had just dropped the daisy cutter. The concussion hit us and because I was precariously bent over picking up a card, it knocked me over.

Not only did we not receive a call that the drop was back on but the wind shifted and it hit on the wrong side of the ridgeline, our side, and we were much closer than the danger close range.

Another incident was after a combat assault outside of Quang Tri. The combat assault was basically uneventful; however, the next couple of nights we were hammered regularly with 61 m.m. mortars by the enemy. They came close to us but never hit us. We had to call in a false location and walk our artillery in close to our location to deter them and make them think we had moved so they would redirect their fire. We were ducking shrapnel from our artillery as well as the enemy's. This was not the first time we had to duck from our own incoming rounds nor was it the last.

A couple of nights later we had set up on a hilltop overlooking the area. When setting up, the forward observer (F.O.) or in our case, "Four Eyes" would plot out defensive targets or "D.T.'s". These were areas that we believed the enemy would be firing mortars or 122 m.m. rockets from. Sometime during the night the N.V.A. launched a barrage of 122's at Quang Tri. As the rockets were fired, "Four Eyes" was on the radio calling a battery of 105 m.m. or 155 m.m. artillery to silence the rockets. It was either luck or good planning but the position was a D.T. plotted earlier in the day. One round was called in for location then it was a battery firing 3 x 3 (6 cannon firing 9 rounds each in a pattern) "for effect". We didn't see any more rockets after that.

"Four Eyes", on left, calling in "D.T.'s" and author, on right, with head showing above log. Lt. Townsend with back to camera.

The next two incidences involve scout teams, which is comprised of a dog and their handler. On occasions we would have them with us as a point team.

The first story is placed here to show why, no matter how tired we were, being careful as well as not being lazy was so important, and the results thereof.

All of us were tired after the day of humping, but that was common. We also had a newby with us, but I remember very little about him except he was an E-7 (Sergeant First Class) and had been with us only a few days. The dog handler had not worked with us before, so I do not know if he had much experience in the bush, but I doubt if he did because of his actions. We had found a suitable place to set up for the night and everyone was picking out a spot to eat or erect their hooches. The newby was bent over his ruck and going through it to pull out some food or possibly items needed to set up for the night. I was in the process of unpacking my poncho and cleaning off a spot to erect my hooch. The dog handler apparently did not like the spot where he had dropped his gear, so he decided to move his ruck and weapon to a new spot. Unfortunately, he did it the wrong way.

Because of the noise factor, to move your ruck, you always picked it up and carried it. The same with your weapon. Even though he was probably tired, I think the handler was just being lazy because he dragged his ruck on the ground to his new spot. He returned for the rest of his gear and proceeded to drag the equipment on the ground. He had his pistol belt in one hand, and was dragging his M-16 with the butt on the ground, while holding the M-16 by the barrel. Which is absolutely the wrong thing to do.

The M-16 apparently snagged on some brush or bushes and discharged. The loud crack from the M-16 being fired got everyone's immediate attention. I do not know if the handler had the safety on or not. Unfortunately, when the M-16 went off, the E-7 was in the line of fire and the bullet struck him in the back. The E-7 was extremely fortunate, for since he was bent over his ruck, the bullet entered near the small of his back and traveled up along his backbone, just barely under the skin. We could see the form of the bullet under the skin, and as near as the medics could tell, he was not seriously injured. Regardless, he had to be medivaced out that night so a medivac chopper was dispatched to extract him. They hovered over our position and lowered a device to pull him up out of the jungle and took him back to the rear. That was also the last time we saw him.

Because of the loud report of the M-16 being fired and the chopper coming in, we had to repack our rucks and hump some more to find another suitable spot to set up for the night. All of this happened because the dog handler was too lazy to do things right! If the E-7 had not been bending over his ruck, he would have been very seriously injured or possibly killed.

The second story is an incident that happened at Eagle beach. There was a handler and his dog with us when we went in. I vaguely remember the handler being in the bush with us but he had more experience than the handler did in the previous incident. The thing I always remember, is the dog.

We had been working near a river or a stream and I can remember we threw empty pop cans into the water for the dog to retrieve. When the dog retrieved the cans, the holes in the cans were large enough that you could almost place your finger in them! But this dog was very smart. Apparently, he had been around the locals before and did not like how they teased or treated him. The Vietnamese looked at most dogs as just another meal. The handler tied the dog to a tree so he would have some shade, and left him food and water. All of us got along with the dog fine, so we would stop by and pet him and give him attention.

The locals however, liked to tease him. But as I said, he was a very smart dog. When you observe an area where a dog is tied to, you can see the limit or length of his chain by the path worn into the ground as it has paced back and forth. When this dog paced back and forth to create a path, he stopped about three feet shorter than the length of his chain. It was irrelevant to us because we got along with the dog and he liked us. Anyway, the dog was starting to get fed up with the locals teasing him, and a Vietnamese girl, probably in her early teens, decided to tease him. So, she stood where the dog had created the boundary of his chain length and started teasing the dog. It was unknown to her that the dog still had three feet of chain left. One of the witnesses said she was taking her finger(s) and "shooting" the dog to tease him. The girl thought she was being smart by teasing the dog from a safe distance, but the dog was smarter than she was and he had had enough of the teasing. He lunged toward her as he still had three feet of chain and bit her in the leg. After the screaming died down and the handler got the dog to let loose of her, the medics had to sew her up. As I said, the dog was very smart.

Dog handler with the dog mentioned above, and Sgt. Wakefield.

The last story in this section relates to defective grenades. We were set up for the night on an L.Z. that we had been on before. It had been resupply day and unfortunately, the supply choppers put us behind so we had to set up where we had been resupplied; something we definitely were against.

We always preferred to put some space between the L.Z. and us because everyone in the area knew where we were. And it doesn't take a rocket scientist to figure out that we probably didn't leave the L.Z. area, as it was almost dark when the last resupply chopper left.

Sometime after dark we could hear noises below us and we assumed we were being probed. There was too much movement and noise for it to be animals. Muzzle flash from an M-16 would give our position away so we decided to lob a few grenades in the area of the noise. This is where the problem began. We had two types of grenades with us. One version we referred to as the "pineapple" style which is similar to the ones you see on TV in WW2 movies except they didn't have the serrations. The other style was the "baseball" style grenade. Unfortunately, the majority of the grenades we had were of the "baseball" type. I think I had only one or two of the "pineapple" style and the rest of mine were the "baseball" type. The first "baseball" grenade was lobbed down the hill, rolled to the ground and did nothing. So did the second, third and so on. Only the "pineapple" grenades went off. I think I threw two of the "baseball" type and neither of them went off. We were obviously quite upset over the situation and I assume the N.V.A. were probably laughing under their breath later that night at the "high quality" American munitions. I would also bet a couple of N.V.A. "soiled" themselves when the dud grenades landed close to them.

The next day we had a chopper bring out a new supply of "pineapple" type grenades and all the "baseball" type we sent to the rear.

Part of the reason for this story being told is to make you wonder or speculate. Can you imagine how you would feel being in a combat zone and everything on your back and all of your ammunition and your weapon were supplied to you by the lowest bidder? Have you ever wondered how many Americans were killed or wounded in action because of defective weapons or munitions? We were very fortunate that night because ultimately, we did not engage the enemy in a firefight. But the final outcome will never be known because the grenades could not be retrieved. Possibly they were made into booby traps or maybe they simply deteriorated during the monsoons. Or another scenario is that, if the first few grenades had exploded; possibly we would have gotten one or two of the enemy, preventing those N.V.A. from killing or wounding G.I.'s later on. It is possible and conceivable that defective American ordinance ultimately created American casualties.

I have heard similar stories relating to both sides in the war. Poorly made Vietnamese grenades (or pipe bombs in some cases) not going off as they landed near a G.I. Also instances of the N.V.A. missing G.I.'s because they were laying on the ground and the banana clip in their AK-47 was too long and they shot over the heads of the G.I.'s.

Stories of this nature always made and still make me wonder about close calls and the close calls we were never aware of. I am sure there were cases or situations where we were within a few yards of the enemy and we never knew it and neither did they.

EATING, CARDS, READING, WRITING, LETTERS FROM HOME AND OTHER THINGS

I have covered the food subject somewhat in the ruck section. Considering everything else, the food we had was quite good. I do not know who developed the freeze-dried food we were carrying but it was excellent. After a long day of humping during the monsoons, it was nice to sit back and open my favorite L.R.R.P. ration and warm the water and myself over the stove. The stove was a "C" ration can that had holes in the side created by a can opener. I would place a blue heating tab inside and light it, set on the canteen cup with water in it and warm it. At the same time we would normally take our poncho liners out and cover the stove and ourselves in an attempt to dry off and warm up. The freeze-dried food would need to rehydrate for a few minutes then we could chow down. The chili con carne was not too popular because it took too long for the beans to soften. Sometimes we just added cold water to the L.R.R.P. rations and ate them. If tired or on the trail, sometimes the freeze-dried foods were eaten dry. Not very tasty but they sufficed. It did make me thirsty though.

The "C" rations or "Charlie rats", as they were often referred to, for the most part weren't too bad either, just heavier to carry. The fruits were always good as well as some of the meats. It was not uncommon to be roasting a ham slice or pork slice with your bayonet over a heating tab and it would fall off to the ground. You would knock off the big pieces of dirt and eat it anyway. Considering the water we drank, it didn't make any difference.

Mixing two to make your own creations was also common. A L.R.R.P. ration of chicken and rice with a can of boned chicken from "C" rations was always a good combo.

As I mentioned in the ruck section we typically carried about ten to twelve days worth of food. When I ordered food for resupply I always ordered more than what we needed. We would pick and choose and load our rucks up. Whatever was left was sent back to the firebase on the last bird out after resupply. The guys at the firebases normally didn't get the L.R.R.P. rations so they thought the chili con carne was great.

Sometimes the ten or twelve days worth of food wasn't enough. I can remember during the monsoons when the choppers couldn't get in because we were socked in, and we ran out of food. We would be down to hot chocolate and coffee and that was all we had. Some would mix the chocolate and coffee together to make it more bearable. Today it is considered a trendy beverage. Then we would lay low for a couple of days to conserve what we had till the slicks could get in. We did have strobe lights to help guide the birds in when they got close, but I can only remember using them once, or maybe twice at the most.

As you are reading this book, somewhere through the pages you might decide to get out of your chair and have a snack. Maybe some potato chips or corn chips, a slice of pizza, a cold glass of milk or orange juice. Maybe you will have an apple or fresh fruit, or maybe just a cold pop or beer and some popcorn. Sounds good doesn't it?

Yes it does, and in 'Nam it also sounded good, except we didn't have any of those. The only one I remember having was from a care package. One of the guys received some jiffy pop and we ate it one night when arriving at a firebase. The milk, juice, cold beverage, and fresh fruit we could have whenever we went to the rear, which was almost never.

For snacks we had cereal bars that came in L.R.R.P. rations. They looked and tasted a lot like finely ground sawdust, but they were edible. We received crackers in cans (b-2 unit), and a small tin of peanut butter, jelly or cheese and that was our snack food. Sometimes we received a package from the rear that contained some candy and other items. I can vaguely remember these packages because of the snacks they contained.

An item we sometimes received on resupply day was some soft drinks and beer. Maybe enough for three to five cans each. We would divide it by who wanted beer or who wanted soft drinks. It helped to offset the taste of the water we had. You also should realize we drank it warm. Whatever the temperature was outside was the temperature of your drink. If it was 100 degrees out, so was the beverage. It was common to take your bayonet and dig a small hole and place a can of beverage in it so it could absorb the cooler ground temperature. My habit was to have a soft drink first thing in the morning. Today I still prefer my Coke for breakfast.

The cans did not have pull-tabs as we think of them today. The Viet Cong was known to take hypodermic needles and inject acid into the cans through the tab, so none of the cans had tabs.

Eating was done somewhat in shifts. There were no rules or guidelines, but normally someone would want to rest their legs before they ate, so they would pull guard while others ate. Also, being as we were quiet we could hear anyone approaching. Setting up at night was also a similar process. We always had to be on defense.

Billy Edwards, "Bull", and the rest of the team, taking a break.

Relaxing, or unwinding as we think of it today, was almost impossible. We tried to take our mind off of the stresses of war for short durations by doing other things. As I have mentioned, cards was a common form of distracting the mind. Someone would be pulling guard (can't drop the defense) while others played cards. Spades was the game "Wild Bill" and I excelled in, Euchre was also played, as well as Hearts. If memory serves me correctly, "TJ"(Tom Johnson) was the king of Hearts. He was very difficult to beat.

Reading was also a way to distract your train of thought. A lot of novels were read and passed around. I believe I read more in 'Nam than in the States. After a long hump I think a telephone book would have been enjoyable to read.

Enjoying a short break with some reading.

Top left: Billy Edwards, "Water Buffalo", and "Wild Bill", reading. The other two are unidentifiable.

We also received the "Stars and Stripes" newspaper that was distributed in 'Nam. It was military published so it was "cleansed" before anything was published in it.

Writing letters home was always a distraction from the war. Most of the troops wrote letters home. Whenever I wrote letters I never mentioned what was going on or how things were. They were almost a form letter. They always started out, "Hi mom, how are things with you and the boys back in the world"? Never a word was mentioned about combat assaults until I hit number 25. Why worry people back home?

The one thing that irritated me was to write someone some letters and they never responded. I figured if I took the time, while sitting in the rain or mud, to write a letter the least they could do was reply. If they could sit in the comfort of their living room eating a pizza and having a cold one while we were in the rain, the least they could do was send a postcard or write a short note. After a few weeks of no response I would quit wasting my time on them.

Letters from home were always good to get. It helped to keep morale up, most of the time. But there were occasions when a letter was received referring to the fact that the wife was leaving her husband or your girlfriend was dumping you, or by the way "I'm pregnant" and you are not the father. Obviously, these letters didn't set well, but as we look back I have to assume we were all better off without the people who wrote them. The letters were being written to the men these people had known in the States. What these people didn't realize was that we had changed or were going through changes and these letters were really written to someone else with the same name. Maybe that statement is an ego thing but I believe we were better off, as well as the writers, because of not being able to deal with us. That statement is probably true today. Besides, that was part of our mindset and being hardcore.

Regarding letters, I can remember receiving mail four days after being mailed in the States. Along with it might be a letter mailed 3 to 4 weeks earlier. As I look back, it is nice to know some things never change.

Also, as I reflect back, the importance of mail back home had many purposes or functions. I was writing to a girl that I had met in Georgia. Her brother was a friend I had met during my O.J.T. at Fort Benning. I believe that one of the reasons the letter writing was so important was for hope or a sense of purpose. It helped sustain a mental drive to get us back home. Whether the purpose was to reunite with the individual or to stay mad at them so you could have a face-to-face argument with them, they served a purpose. I know we didn't write them to tell what we were really doing. I don't know anyone in Recon that did.

As you reminisce with a 'Nam vet, some faded or wrinkled pictures may be pulled out of a drawer or scrapbook for you to look at. Handle them with care for usually there aren't any negatives and they may be the only tangible memories he can hold and look at.

Picture-taking in 'Nam doesn't match the vision of picture-taking today. First of all, we needed film and a camera. Being as we didn't go to the rear very often, most of the time we didn't have film. When someone went to the rear they would bring back a lot of film for the others. We would set up times when we could pose with a friend or two, but if you notice, most posed photos are in the rear and people are able to smile for a moment. The best shots are those that are missed. Can you imagine the problems we would have had trying to take pictures as we were going in for a combat assault! A good camera was hard to find in the bush and also hard to carry, as space in the ruck was at a premium. The smaller or more compact the camera, the better. The camera I had for many months broke and was held together with rubber bands before it was stolen when we were on Co Pung. When someone took pictures, extra copies were made for those who didn't have a camera or film.

When "Wild Bill" and I met again, after 28 years, we were comparing pictures we had. The ones of Co Pung were the same! Several months later, when we reunited with Howie and Gary, Howie also had the same pictures of Co Pung. Howie probably snapped the photos and passed the extras around (thanks Howie).

As I mention film I should also mention money. We were paid in "script" or money printed by the military. We did not have pocket change, as all the coin values were paper. Green backs or U.S. currency was illegal there until the very end.

In the bush you didn't need money except for film, having pictures developed, or a couple of odds and ends. The few times we went to the rear some money was needed for beverage and etc., but not much. Mainly you saved your money in a savings account and only needed it for an R&R. Postage for letters home was free and in place of a stamp the word "free" was penciled in.

STANDDOWN, THE REAR AND OLD FRIENDS

A standdown was something everyone was to partake in on a regular basis. A standdown was a way to let go and not worry for a few days. Many units were in the jungle for a week and went to the rear for one to two weeks. Some units, instead of coming in to the rear might go to a firebase for a few days of less stressful environment.

A standdown was supposed to be like a weekend off or spring break. Stop what we were doing, relax, forget about everything else and catch a movie. Many times it was a chance to go to the P.X. (Post Exchange) and buy stationary, candy, film, have film developed, or whatever.

The concept of a standdown was to have a chance to shower, get clean clothes, dry off and warm up (if it was the monsoons), prepare for the next mission, unwind, or get drunk as many G.I.'s did.

According to an old timer from California that was in Recon in 1966 & 1967, the O'Deuce Recon platoon, when under Headquarters Company, was out for a week and in for two.

Unfortunately, rare was the day that we were out of the bush for a standdown. Thanksgiving was three or four days and I believe Christmas was eleven days. I can remember those because of new faces coming in and because of the holidays and length of them. Also I remember these because they accounted for over one half of the time I was out of the bush during my stint in the Recon platoon.

Part of the Recon platoon waiting for a ride to the Bob Hope show: author is on far left.

Another group of Recon men headed to the Bob Hope show.

View of the crowd behind Recon. Lt. Bridges is in center left, talking to two Generals.

Typically, there would be some form of entertainment, whether it was live or a movie. Many times problems arose because the Recon platoon had the front row reserved for them in the open-air theater area and we would often disrupt the entertainment. Either because someone had too much to drink, or what we were drinking out of (human skulls, more on that later), or because it had been so long since we had come out of the jungle, that we were just being rowdy. Often times the Line Companies gave Recon a hard time because we did have reserved seats.

Because of the rarity of getting out of the bush, many of the Recon men got drunk as skunks. They were totally plastered because there was so much tension and stress to get rid of that drinking was the only outlet they knew of to relieve themselves of some stress.

I can remember a couple of times that "Four Eyes" handed me his wallet after he had removed enough money from it for drinking, and instructing me not to give it back to him until we were on the chopper pad heading back to the bush.

Being as I was and still am a non-drinker, I would try to unwind by catching up on my writing or read a book, as did several others.

There was a lot of drug use in 'Nam but it was not tolerated by Recon.

We had to depend on each other too much for any chemical dependency problems.

I believe it was after our ninety plus days in the bush when we did come in, that some of the guys were drinking or drunk for the whole time we were in. When the standdown was over, so was the drinking.

The one standdown that stands out in my mind was a trip to Eagle beach. The other team had set an ambush that resulted in three N.V.A. being taken out plus it yielded quite a bit of intelligence. As a result, both teams were sent into Eagle beach for a break. The thing I always remember was standing in chow line and hearing the song "Out in the Country" by Three Dog Night. It seemed so appropriate and relaxing for the situation. Every time I hear the song today, it puts me back at Eagle beach, standing in chow line.

Doc Hardee and Doc McGuire (standing), Harry Hardin, Jim Turnbull, Hector Martinez (seated) at Eagle Beach.

Billy Campbell on left and Dan "OD" O'Doughtery.

Billy Edwards and Jim "Bull" Turnbull.

To add a little humor to this chapter, one night when we were in on a standdown, we were doing the usual of playing some cards and sipping on sodas or beer. We were in one of the barracks enjoying ourselves being we were warm, dry, had a full stomach and no one was shooting at us. There was only one problem: one of the Recon men had unwound too much. He had gotten drunk, which was not uncommon in the rear, but he was also snoring like a horse. He was snoring so loudly that we could not enjoy ourselves. We tried everything we could think of to get him to stop, but nothing worked. So, out of despair, I took a piece of garlic salami that I had (I believe Lt. Townsend had given it to me) and cut off a chunk of it, to prop his mouth open in order to end his snoring. Needless to say, it worked. There was only one drawback. All of us went to bed and forgot about taking it out, so he slept with the garlic salami in his mouth and breathed through his mouth all night long! We went back out to the field the next day, and for the next day or two he complained about the garlic taste in his mouth that he could not get rid of and he couldn't figure out how he had gotten it. I don't think anyone ever told him either.

I would like to add more on stand-downs, but being they were so rare, there is a lack of memories on them.

One of the interesting events of being in the rear, or really anywhere in 'Nam, was running into old friends or people who knew of mutual friends.

I can remember an occasion of being in the rear and waiting in the chow line. It was something I did not like to do because everyone stood too close together. I think it was the Christmas cease-fire but I am not positive. Anyway, as I was standing in line a soldier walked by and I gave him a funny look because I thought I knew him. As it turned out, I did. I had run around with him some when I lived in Indiana, prior to going in the Army, and we also had mutual friends.

When I was in the South in the 25th Infantry, I had similar experiences. People always asked what state you were from and then what part of the State. In one instance, a soldier from another company mentioned that he knew of another soldier from the same area. It turned out to be another person that I used to cruise around with. And coincidentally, he also knew the old friend I met later in the 101st.

I have heard dozens of similar stories from other vets. They may have been in the rear, on an R&R, an L.Z., or almost anywhere you can think of when they met. Many of the soldiers wore the name of their hometown on their boonie cap, which always tipped off other soldiers of their origin.

There is only one thing wrong with all the stories of friends meeting friends in Viet Nam. It is a sign that we had too many young men there.

NICKNAMES, CODES AND RULES

As you have noticed by now, almost everyone had a nickname, (all Lieutenants were simply known as "LT."), "Marty", "Four Eyes", "Wild Bill", "Pappy", "Water Buffalo", "Bull", "Firetruck", "OD", "Hogbody", "TJ", "Lambchops", "Smitty", "Mabby", "Doc", and "Doc Shaky", just to name a few.

The assignment of a nickname had several advantages and functions.

First of all, it indicated respect from your comrades when your nickname was used over your real name. You were now established.

Secondly, it reflected upon one's heritage, personality or initials. "Four Eyes" wore glasses, "Water Buffalo" looked bulky, "Doc Shaky" didn't have the steadiest hands, "Wild Bill" looked like a wild Bill, "Firetruck's" dad was a fireman, "OD" was short for O'Doughtery, and I had mutton chop sideburns, etc, etc. It was also easier than remembering their real name.

Often times people didn't know your real name, only the nickname. As I reflect back on this, it may have been a mental device or tool in case one of us didn't make it back. The nickname created an imaginary space between the real individual and us. If we lost someone, then we lost a nickname, not a man. That way, no one really knew anyone else. It may have been sort of a coping mechanism to deal with the horrors of war.

The primary reason was for use on the radio. The North Vietnamese and Viet Cong were great at propaganda. If your real name was spoken in the clear there were chances that a letter may be received back home depicting your demise or some other obscene comments.

Radio procedure required coding (by using S.O.I.'s) information and other procedures that slowed down radio communications. It was easier to pick up the radio and rattle off nicknames and other jargon to communicate with, than to go secure on the Delta-1 radio. Besides, the Delta-1 was not always perfect and often times was "all squelch". It was also primarily for use in communications with battalion. Not only that, but we only had one radio that could go "secure" and the other 2 were PRC-25's so we had to devise alternative languages. And really, talking effectively on the radio in the "clear" had many advantages. For one, we were speaking in a language only we understood. Not only that, it was often times fun to create our own vocabulary, plus it kept everyone guessing, who didn't understand what we were saying. You could call it planned confusion or playing mind games, but regardless, it helped keep us alive.

We did use the standard terminology as everyone else for calling in a fire mission for support, or helicopter language for smoke, gunships, and etc. but even the enemy knew these. As a matter of fact, they probably knew them better than we did.

It was also a huge advantage in keeping the enemy confused. We knew they listened in to our transmissions so we often created conversations to keep them off balance. As I mentioned earlier, war is a big game of hide and seek but fought with guns. We hid and we also sought. The trick was to keep the enemy, and sometimes our commanders, confused on our location and strength. The more confused the enemy was about us, the better our odds of survival were. Sometimes our Battalion Commander was believed to be the enemy due to his inexperience and inability. Most people I mention by name or nickname whenever possible in this book. The first Battalion Commander we had was a Lt. Colonel nicknamed "Shamrock", as he preferred to be called (no reference to rank!). He was well respected by all. The next Battalion Commander we had (referred to as Lt. Col. "X"), because of his lack of ability and experience, deserved no respect so therefore his name will not be mentioned in this book.

A primary key to our survival was not allowing anyone outside of our group to know exactly where we were all the time. It allowed us to create the illusion of moving in the night, when in reality, all we did was claim to move and no one could prove otherwise.

"Wild Bill" and I often communicated on the radio and we did pretty well at creating our own language. On one particular occasion we were creating diversion by referring to ourselves as company R.T.O.'s instead of the team-sized units we were in. One of us was Foxtrot or "F" company (coincidentally, my DD-214 shows me as being in "F" company when in 'Nam, and "F" company never existed) and the other was Golf or "G" company (it didn't exist either). We conversed on subjects that neither of us can remember, but were most likely focused on two companies having an operation and tactics being used. Regardless of the conversation, the outcome had excellent results. It saved our lives.

As the story was told to me by "Wild Bill" in 1998, the Recon platoon had taken a couple of prisoners. This was right after I was kicked out of the field (more on this later) and sent to the rear. During the interrogation the prisoners wanted to know about the strength or size of "Foxtrot" and "Golf" companies. They had plans on ambushing or attacking the Recon platoon (approximately 20 to 24 of us), but they held back because they figured they were outnumbered and outgunned because of the two other Line Companies. They had our numbers placed at over 200 men because of the conversation between the two "company" R.T.O.'s: "Wild Bill" and myself.

I know of other vets who have told similar stories of having fake conversations or playing games over the airwaves to keep the enemy off balance.

Even today the nicknames still stick with us, even if we are the only ones who understand the meanings or reasons behind them.

When I mention names like "Smitty" and Lt. Townsend, I remember the nickname but I cannot remember their first names. But this is not unusual. The first time I called "Wild Bill" to find out if he was the Don Corey I knew from Vietnam, he didn't know who I was, until I said "Lambchops" and then he immediately knew who I was and had a visual picture of me. A few minutes into the conversation he was looking at pictures of us taken in 'Nam, as was I.

The heading for this segment was "Nicknames, Codes, and Rules".

Here is a listing of our rules for engagement, calling in artillery, and everything else:

1.
2.
3.
4.
5.
6.
7.
8.
9.
10.

There were none! We didn't believe in them.

We were given the usual "guidelines" or rules as referred to by the Army but we knew that the enemy also knew our "guidelines" and used them to their advantage. So why should we use them?

Our only goal was to survive, nothing more, nothing less, and if we created our own radio language, why not create our own rules?

Some other advantages we had over Line Companies were targets of engagement and free fire zones. In certain areas curfews were in place and there were rules of engagement. In the case of the Recon platoon, anyone at any time was fair game. All our areas were freefire or we didn't go in.

The Recon platoon, in later months, was famous for making "quick" night moves to throw the enemy off balance or off guard. A night move is at best dangerous and risky. A night move is picking up all your gear in the middle of the night and relocating to evade enemy mortar attacks or other indirect fire. So why take unnecessary chances to prove a point? It goes back to my earlier comment; don't always tell everyone where we are, or if we do, claim we moved and don't tell anyone that we didn't. It kept everyone else off balance.

Incoming mortar fire was a common, nightly occurrence in certain areas. This was often referred to as H & I fire or harassment and interdiction. The enemy was simply trying to nail us with 61m.m. mortars. These rounds had a maximum range of about 600 meters, and they knew that we could not call artillery within 1000 meters of our location, so they felt safe knowing we could not retaliate when they got close. And how did they know when they got close? Because when they got too close, we called in artillery. With a map and some logic they could guess our approximate location by where we placed return fire. But as with Foxtrot and Golf companies, we called in to battalion and gave new grid coordinates because we had just completed a "quick night move" to evade the enemy mortars. The N.V.A. was also listening to our transmissions along with the firebase. Everyone, including the enemy, knew we had moved (although we had not) so their thought process of where we had moved to started, and the rounds began dropping in a different area. The firebase would also receive clearance from the Battalion Commanding Officer because we were now out of "danger close" range and they would start dropping artillery on the enemy.

They knew our rules as well as we did, so they looked on their maps, figured out where we might have moved to, and started placing mortars in a new location. All that time we were ducking from shrapnel from our own incoming artillery rounds, while letting the North Vietnamese and our superiors think we had moved in the middle of the night, and proving our superior soldier techniques. Also, we hopefully were reducing the enemy population while improving our chances for survival. We never had to call artillery directly on top of us, but we called it awful damned close on occasions and you couldn't have gotten a blade of grass or a hair between the ground and us. It is amazing how close you can make your body conform to the shape of the ground when needed. And you need to remember that we did not have shovels to dig holes with.

There were a couple of instances when this was a little more difficult to pull off because we were out of support range. With the N.V.A. not receiving return fire from our artillery, we had to sound winded or like we were moving to make the illusion work. It took more radio conversation to convince everyone on both sides we had moved before the North Vietnamese diverted their fire to another grid location.

This is also an indicator of where we were or weren't. We had to be a long way out, to be out of artillery range, and sometimes we had difficulty raising someone on the radio. Even putting up the long antennae didn't always bring in communications.

One "rule" that was our own, and one that we lived by or we died by because we did not obey it, was noise discipline. Noise discipline is a simple rule: no noise. This may sound easy but it is difficult to go days, weeks, or months without talking in normal tones and volumes. Silence is golden! We whispered all the time. This included the Foxtrot and Golf Company scenarios mentioned earlier, any and all radio conversations or transmissions, playing cards, and any normal conversations were whispered.

During patrols, or the teams or platoon moving, we whispered and used hand signals. We used tape on our rucks so they didn't make noise. As we packed our rucks, everything was placed so it didn't rattle or squeak.

When we ate we made sure that open "C" ration cans weren't dropped. Our "cooking" stove was a "C" ration can and we took special care as we placed our canteen cup on it so it didn't make noise. And after enjoying (?) the warm can of pop or beer that we occasionally had, there was no belching! Eating, drinking, and sleeping, were all done quietly. Snoring was obviously taboo and I do not remember anyone having a snoring problem in the bush. I think in order to snore you needed to be in a deeper sleep than we acquired.

Most grunts in Line Companies carried a small shovel called an e-tool (entrenching tool) so they could dig a foxhole at night. We didn't "dig in" because it made noise, and shovels were also noisemakers while being carried. Being metal, they could clang or make other loud noises as we humped. In place of carrying a shovel or e-tool we used a "C" ration can to take care of burying our private business.

Steel pots or helmets were standard in Line Companies. We never saw one! We wore a "boonie" hat made of cloth because it didn't make any noise.

It was common for grunts in Line Companies to have transistor radios so they could listen to music. Why not! They talked, laughed, and dug in nightly- why not a little more noise?

Some Line Companies used air mattresses but they were also noisemakers when you rolled. We slept on the hard ground.

Another drawback of whispering was long-term enunciation. After whispering for a day, try and talk normal. Imagine what it would be like if you whispered for two or three weeks straight.

Even today, it still affects us. When I am tired I slur badly, and my enunciation is poor. I have had conversations in recent months with "Four Eyes" when we were both tired and it was almost comical because neither of us could talk straight.

The only time we actually talked in the field was during extractions or as the birds were coming in to extract us.

Another item that is appropriate to place here even though it is not noise related is smoking. Smoking was restricted to daylight hours. If it were approaching darkness, some people would finish smoking their cigarette backwards. That is, lit portion inside their mouth! A cigarette being lit or smoked after dark could easily compromise our position.

THE EYES TELL IT ALL

Hector "Marty" Martinez was considered a newby to the Recon platoon during the Christmas standdown. This is obvious by the pictures of us. Some snapshots of several of us were taken while we waited for a ride to the Bob Hope show. In the pictures all one has to do is to look into the eyes to tell if a soldier was an old timer or a newby. The eyes tell it all! "Marty's" eyes still had some twinkle or hint of innocence, maybe a little smile or a grin on his face. There was expression or emotion showing on his face and in his eyes. There were also a couple of other guys ("Hogbody" and "O.D".) that were also newbys, and it shows in their faces as well.

Doc Edwards, Dan O'Doughtery, James Patrick, Hector Martinez, Bob Groetsema. Notice the smiles on their faces and the twinkle in their eyes.

The author. Notice the blank stare in the eyes.

An old timer or one with combat or field experience is easy to pick out. Look into their eyes and there is a blank, solemn, expressionless, emotionless, cold stare that goes to their very soul…. if they have one left. You can almost look right through them. The stare or faraway look seems to run forever, and often times it did. Sometimes the look will give you the impression that "nobody is home", and at that point, probably nobody was. The experience of what that person had dealt with or was dealing with was probably more than God had ever planned on him seeing or doing, and it showed; or in this case, nothing showed. The eyes are telling you that he had seen more than he wanted to see and done more than he wanted to do. To cope with the effects he had become or was becoming hardcore. You can see it in his eyes! The eyes are telling you that he needed space and someone to understand him; not a sneer saying, "nobody is home"! We were that way in 'Nam and many of us are still that way today. We are still dealing with what we saw or did and our eyes are telling you that.

The next time you have a discussion with a friend or family member and the conversation is full of emotion, look into their eyes and you can almost understand what is being said by reading their eyes. The emotion of the eyes will tell you a story, but the eyes of a combat vet will tell you a different story and it is one of pain, of sadness, of hardships, of friends lost, and of the horrors he has seen. The faraway look in his eyes is telling you the story that he has been damaged or terrified beyond what the average person could begin to imagine or deal with. That he has done things he couldn't believe he could do, or ever wants to do again. They are telling you that he has experienced the highs and lows of combat assaults and firefights, of friends injured or killed, and other horrors of war. If you look at a blank wall or blank blackboard all they tell you is nothing. On a combat vet, blank eyes will tell you a lot; you just have to know how to read them.

If you ever talk in confidence to a 'Nam vet and war stories are being told you can always tell who the grunts or combat soldiers are. The eyes will always tell the story. When he starts to tell the story there will be some form of a faraway look in his eyes and his voice will become monotone. As he speaks, his voice will often crack or become raspy as he struggles to put the words into motion. There won't be any smiles or chuckles. As you listen to his story carefully, do not judge his comments or actions. He was there and you weren't. He is trying to explain a situation that seemed like it happened yesterday but was really thirty years ago or more and it helped to create that faraway look in his eyes. As you listen, try to place yourself there and try to understand the conditions. You are doing him a favor by listening and doing yourself some good because you are starting to understand him. After the event has been replayed for you, ask yourself if you would not have problems doing what he did or seeing what he saw.

A R.E.M.F. (rear echelon mother f***er) will laugh or smile as he relates his story with a twinkle in his eyes. Odds are the story is exaggerated or belongs to someone else. The combat soldier who has been in the bush for any length of time considers the R.E.M.F. and dog feces as being on the same level or being of equal value.

Look at any pictures of a 'Nam vet who was in the field for any duration and notice his eyes. You'll realize that he is not smiling from ear to ear. The faraway look tells you that he has seen more or done more than he ever wanted to see and do. And most of the time they did not choose to be there. Most of the grunts were doing their patriotic duty, a price we paid for living in a place called the United States. The next time you are in a place where you are saying " I pledge allegiance to the flag of the United States of America and to the Republic for which it stands", remember why a vet has the faraway stare in his eyes. Also remember that it is because of the vets that you can stand and pledge allegiance!

When I was leaving 'Nam, I ran across an old friend that I was in basic training with at Fort Knox, Kentucky. Larry and I were in the same barracks, being his last name started with an R. He was always smiling and typically easy going. He was just a decent guy that was pleasant to be around. I am assuming he extended his time in 'Nam because he would have arrived approximately 6 months before I did, as I had gone to N.C.O. School. As I talked to him,

I realized very quickly that he had a very rough time in 'Nam. He had the monotone voice and that faraway stare in his eyes. He wasn't smiling or even excited about going home. He was just there, an empty shell. No more smiles or easygoing attitude; he had seen more or done more than he could handle and his eyes told it all.

Another thing, when looking into the eyes, is notice the unemotional look or coldness there. The lack of emotion is seen in the eyes and transgresses throughout the brain. Being hardcore, and seeing things or doing the things we did, a person becomes numb to events that bother others. We have a conscience, but not the feelings connected to emotion. We had to detach the emotional strings we had in order to mentally survive seeing people wounded, mutilated, or killed. Part of being hardcore is losing emotional ties with the brain. As you read this book, there are many references to lack of emotion and being hardcore. It did not bother us to drink out of a fresh human skull. Most people were appalled by it because of emotion. To us, it was a regular drinking vessel. I don't think I can over-emphasize how much we had to lose our emotional attachments to cope with what we were going through. If we hadn't detached ourselves mentally, we would have been basket cases or in worse shape than we are today.

The highs and lows of combat assaults drive emotions away. After the roller coaster ride in the helicopter and not knowing if you will live another minute longer, or will see tomorrow makes drinking out of a human skull irrelevant.

We carried bodies from crashed helicopters, enduring the blood and goriness of it all. Does showing emotion help us cope, or does becoming harder and harder make it easier?

Every combat assault, mortar attack, firefight, environmental factors, the ruck; every time these events occurred or confronted us, was really just another immunization shot to increase the level of being hardcore and emotionless. That is what their eyes are telling you. "I have seen more or done more than I ever wanted to do!" The only way I could handle it was to become hardcore and emotionless. I had to mentally detach myself from the realities of life due to war. That is why I reflect a blank stare as if there was no one home; and often times, no one is home! For me to cope with it, part of me had to leave, and that part of me will probably never come back.

HARDCORE

This is probably as good a spot as any to try and define the term "hardcore". To me, there are two types of hardcore, physical and mental. And really, this is a primary basis for this book. The "Eyes Tell It All" chapter defines the appearance of being hardcore. This defines how we got there. Once a person understands the definitions of hardcore, what transpired to cause us to arrive at that state of mind, and the results there of, then there can be some understanding of why 'Nam vets act or react the way we do. Maybe the correct line is why we don't act or react the way a society of "normal" people, who judge our reactions, think we should.

Being hardcore is not a social status or privilege: it was and still is, part of the survival skills needed to exist. Hardcore is a combination of many ingredients. And remember, none of us asked to become hardcore. I also need to make a clarification here in order to help you understand my comments. Throughout this chapter and this book I refer to the state of being hardcore controlling me. The only analogy I can make to help you understand this comment is this: it is a similar reaction to ducking, flinching, or hitting the brakes when you are driving. These reactions are automatic; you do not think about hitting the brakes when a car pulls out in front of you nor do you think about moving your head when something comes too close. It is automatic and the hardcore state of mind is similar. I fully believe the hardcore state of mind is also a more powerful, or stronger mental reaction than is ducking or hitting the brakes. I say this because I carry and react in a hardcore state of mind 100% of the time, where the other comparisons are lightly used reactions.

The physical aspects of hardcore have been touched on in the topic of "The Ruck" and "The Hump". Regrettably, this is only part of the physical portion of being hardcore. The ruck is a very unforgiving beast that is also a basic lifeline of supplies. I have never had pleasant memories of my ruck. I carried it religiously but I hated it. We all needed every ounce of whatever we carried in or on it, but we also despised having to get on all fours to stand up. Slipping and sliding up and down mountainsides or trails with a ruck never conjures up memories of an enjoyable time. Back aches, leg cramps, sore shoulders and every muscle in your body aching never brings back pleasant memories

But, the physical portion of being hardcore has only been touched. So far the subject has focused on inertia or gravity. What goes up must, come down.

The environment is just as difficult, if not more so. It is very hard to vote on which is number 1 on the scale of discomfort. Weight is tough on the body, but so is temperature.

The monsoons, or 'soons as they are often referred to, create unbearable circumstances, worse than the summer in my opinion. The vast majority of civilians I have talked to think of Vietnam as a hot, steamy jungle, which is true part of the time. Saying that putting up with the heat was not easy, is putting it mildly. Days when the temperature soared above 100 degrees, our fatigues were soaked with sweat, and there was heat exhaustion and running out of water. We were dirty and gross smelling. The summer sun complicates so many things, but, the 'soons were worse.

In the heat of the day we would stop and have some food or play cards. This is when "Wild Bill" and I became so good at playing Spades. A deck of cards was probably twice as thick as normal because of the humidity. Most patrols or recons were in the morning or late afternoon. We would either move in the morning and patrol in the afternoon, or patrol in the morning and move in the afternoon. The activities of the North Vietnamese and Viet Cong were like ours. Even though they were native to the land, they typically kept their movement minimal during the heat of the day. Sweat could be running off of us as if we were in a shower. Of course, we would eventually dry off and smell worse than we already did. After several days of this we were quite ripe, but so was everyone else, so it didn't really matter. Also, in the heat of the day we could typically find some shade and cool off to some degree. But as I mentioned; the 'soons were worse. The one good aspect of the hot weather is you don't slip and slide in mud.

Surviving the summer heat is not an easy task. You also have to remember this is not a day at the beach. Shirts must stay on and buttoned. A shiny chest or back is a great target. Can you imagine trying to hump that monster of a ruck around on a sun burnt back? I did on one occasion after a couple of days in the rear. It wasn't an especially pleasant experience as the 120 pounds bounced on my tender back and the straps persistently cut into my raw shoulders. I always left my shirt on after that when we went to the rear, which was a rare event. We never wore sunglasses because of glare reduction, nor did we even have them. We needed to see any and every reflection because it may be an AK-47 pointed our way or a possible booby trap. We needed every edge or advantage to make it to the next minute and next hour. Suntan lotions and anything else that created odors made us easier targets to find, so we didn't use them.

Surviving the environment was sometimes more difficult than the war. We were always at the ready for a firefight regardless of the situation, but we also had to live in the environment 24 hours a day, 7 days a week. At least we could alternate guard time and take breaks from the heat and sweat. Playing

Spades or having a L.R.R.P. ration allowed us time to divert our thinking from the stress of the bush and the heat of the day. But, the monsoons were worse!

So, you keep asking yourself what can be worse that humping 120 pounds up and down mountains, sweating like a pig, and contending with heat exhaustion? Cold, muddy and wet! The most miserable environment to be in is the 'soons. I can only attempt to explain the monsoon environment but I have to emphasize that no matter how clear the understanding is, it is 10 times worse unless you have experienced it.

Tom "TJ" Johnson, Gary "Four Eyes" Taylor, the author, and Hector "Marty" Martinez at a firebase during the monsoons. Notice the clothing; the temperature is probably between 50 degrees and 55 degrees. Also notice the mud is everywhere.

You have to start with the clothing. Jungle pants, jungle shirt, sometimes a t-shirt, sometimes a nightshirt that is similar to a long sleeved pull over shirt, worn boots and socks. And all these articles of clothing you have been wearing wet for ten days or so and that's it! Underwear was a rarity and was uncomfortable to wear so we didn't wear any. Rain gear in the form of a jacket or anything to keep the rain off of us was unheard of and forbidden. I did have the remains of a raincoat but it was to keep the PRC-77 radio dry. Ponchos were to sleep under, not to wear. I have heard stories of field jackets in Line Companies to keep warm with, but in Recon they did not exist. Of the five of us that have reunited, none of us can remember ever being colder in our lives than in 'Nam during the monsoons.

It is raining out and it has been raining for three weeks straight. We had the same clothes on for the past 10 days and it was 10 days before that when we had a chance to wash our faces off in a cold stream. The temperature is around 50 degrees outside. In the mornings we can see our breath in the damp fog that is hugging the ground. We are wet about 22 hours a day, and cold to the bone even longer. The only time we are dry is early in the morning. And that time coincides with the time we needed to relieve our bladders; which is also the time the leg cramps are preparing to announce their arrival by unleashing their fury. But, we are only dry if the spot we picked to sleep in didn't become a small stream in the middle of the night, or the water found a route to us, which was not uncommon.

Under my poncho, I bundle up with a poncho liner and my M-16. This was how or when I became friends with Gary. As with a lot of the Recon guys, two men would set up together nightly to help reduce the hassle of setting up at nights. Gary and I slept back to back for many, many weeks just to stay warm. But it wasn't unusual to wake up wet from water running into or under the ponchos. As stated earlier, we slept on the ground with part of a poncho under us. Some Line Companies had air mattresses, but they made too much noise and noise was one of our worst enemies. Besides, we are hardcore, remember?

Most of the time during the 'soons we were in the mountains at the higher elevations, so we had the wind to contend with as well as the cold.

Knowing the range of the radios and artillery placed us in the A Shau Valley area and possibly west of the A Shau, which would place us in or near Laos on occasions.

Wet and cold to the bone, it is 50 degrees in the mountains, and not much clothing. Are you getting the picture? Can you imagine how you would feel when, after sleeping on the ground or in mud, you awaken to a cold wet morning knowing that a 100 to 120-pound ruck is waiting for you and you are going to get wet for the 20th, 30th or 40th consecutive day? And while you were sleeping you had guard duty to pull and were sleeping with "one eye open". More on the "one eye open" comment later. You also know that you have to be ready for a firefight at a blink of an eye while you are wet and cold. You also quietly think to yourself that this might be your last day alive, especially if you are preparing to go on a combat assault.

Oh, have I mentioned the leeches yet? These little critters loved to crawl on our bodies, trying to find a warm spot to suck blood from. Fortunately, my body chemistry is acidic. Any watch I have owned has been corroded to some degree. I think this helped to reduce my leech problem. I had my share on me, but nothing compared to others in the Recon platoon. These tough skinned little critters created or could create a lot of problems. The most common way to get rid of these things was to put a dot or two of insect repellent on them and they would curl up and drop off. Salt also worked well if we didn't have bug juice. At night it was hard to find the bug juice, so the typical hardcore method of removing them was to put them in your mouth and chew them in half. Not a pleasant thought, but it was an effective way to eliminate the little bastards. Some people had leeches trying to crawl into their penis or rectum, which would have created big problems if they had completed their journey.

I remember the 8-mile hump we had. It was a real horror of a hump. One of the guys was Alton Mabb. We called him "Mabby" for short. It seemed to me that "Mabby" was a leech magnet. For some reason they were attracted to him more so than others. During the eight-mile hump I believe he walked point part of the time. Upon arriving at the firebase we went into some bunkers to rest for the night. "Mabby" had picked up a couple of leeches during the hump and they had anchored themselves to his neck and had a feast. I can remember those things when they hit the floor after being removed from his neck. They fell and hit with a thud. Seems to me they were about the size of my thumb.

During our time in the bush we typically wore leech straps. These straps were worn at the ankle and just below the knee. They were snug enough to keep leeches from climbing up our pants, but didn't reduce any blood circulation.

The author at an NDP. Shows leech straps just below knee, radio and Delta 1
set up and poncho liner.

Another factor in the equation of being hardcore was combat assaults. I
will only touch briefly on them here because I have a separate chapter on them.
Being in the bush was mentally tough, especially during the monsoons. But
undoubtedly the combat assaults took a very, very heavy toll on us mentally.
Not knowing if we would live through the assault; the highs and lows associated
with the extraction and insertion. Knowing that our bird could easily be shot
down during these situations or a bird in our assault could go down and we
would have to search the wreckage. Knowing that as we went in, we could be
taking our last breath!

I think combat assaults were mentally harder than firefights. A firefight
was normally a brief exchange of gunfire with the enemy, and in our case, we
always initiated it. We had very few firefights but a lot of combat assaults. Plus
combat assaults lasted longer because we had more time to think about them,
and the insertion was riskier because we could not shoot back until we were on
the ground. And when we hit the ground, we were easy targets at first because
there may only be four or five people on the ground until the next bird landed.

Being as I was always on the first bird in, I was always one of the first ones on the ground. Regardless, neither situation was considered any fun. They are both tremendous highs and lows in a very short period of time.

There is a situation that fits in here better than anywhere else and is a defining statement of how hardcore we were and what extremes we went to in surviving. In the chapter on "Rules" I mentioned how we deceived the enemy and our Commanding Officers in that we had moved in the middle of the night to get our artillery called in closer. This was a technique to try and eliminate the enemy and save ourselves by bringing artillery rounds too close to our position; much closer than military rules and guidelines would ever allow.

I am sure everyone has seen a movie where you could hear the artillery round "whistling" during its descent just before it slams into the ground with a deafening explosion. The real thing is much scarier, whether it was from the N.V.A. or it was ours. A person cannot imagine what is going through your head as you hear the whistling of the round coming in, and you know that in this case it is yours! The feeling or emotion, when you are ducking from your own shrapnel and hoping the rounds aren't too close is something I cannot explain on paper. You hear the whistle, hear the round slam into the ground and explode, and the ground under you is also moving or moving you as shrapnel is whizzing over you. If a person weren't hardcore after that situation, they would be a basket case. Whether you were ducking from the N.V.A.'s indirect fire or ours, it was tough on the brain. The scariest time was when you hear the whistling of the round and not knowing how close it was going to hit and explode!

There were areas we were in that we received incoming rounds nightly from the N.V.A. It might only be four to five rounds or twenty-five rounds. Maybe they were missing us by a mile or only 50 meters or less. Regardless, it was a mentally draining event that we can never forget. When it was over we felt like zombies, very dazed and wiped out, to say the least. And when things settled down, it was time to sleep (with one eye open).

Another of the factors of defining hardcore is water. This probably crosses over into the mental portion of hardcore, but this is a good place to elaborate on the water supply. Regardless of what we did, we needed water. Today we all take water for granted. Go to a faucet and out it comes. Not quite that easy in 'Nam.

During the 'soons water was collected off the ponchos (hooches) by using our canteen cups. So we didn't need to carry as much water as in the summer. This probably is the only good detail or factor I can think of relating to the monsoon season. But there were drawbacks; we didn't know how clean the water was. Water being collected off of hooches during a rain would be clean, one would think. Unfortunately, the U.S. had a vision of defoliating the jungle with a "safe" compound called Agent Orange. So every time it rained and we caught water in our canteen cups, we were probably collecting small amounts of Agent Orange for our personal consumption.

The water during the hot months could really be nasty. To begin with, warm water doesn't exactly quench your thirst. Not like an ice-cold soda or beer. Being as rain wasn't common during the summer and we couldn't collect it off our hooches, we had to find other collection devices. Streams were a common collection point but some of the water was so grungy it was unreal. I recall many occasions when we took water from streams with our canteen cups and we couldn't see the bottom of the cup with only an inch or so of water in the cup. This stuff we called water was very nasty stuff. During scarcer times, bomb craters or mud puddles were common sources for water. Again, not very tasty but it sufficed. It took a lot of will power to drink that stuff. When that is all you have, then it has to suffice. What else could we do?

Howard "Pappy" Grabill filling his canteen from a stream.

And for those reading this and thinking, aha, water purification tablets fixed that problem, right? Wrong, I understand our medics had the tablets for those who wanted or needed them, but I don't personally remember seeing them and I know I never used one, nor did the others I was with. And even if we had used them, they would have given only minor results. They were made to treat minor amounts of bacteria or impurities in the water. The levels of bacteria were far higher than they were designed for. They were also not developed to remove or nullify chemicals as Agent Orange and other compounds in the water. We even had a time or two that we had a blivet dropped in during a resupply so we could have water.

The water related aspect of hardcore is somewhat of a physical and mental mixture: physical is to endure drinking it and the mental is convincing yourself to drink it.

Another thought in the factor of being hardcore, was health. You would think drinking all that nasty water would make everyone sick. Being as it was probably full of bacteria, possibly animal and human waste, decaying vegetation, possible chemical contamination, and maybe decaying bodies. It is surprising that we weren't. No doubt that the water gave all of us diarrhea from time to time but that was about it. I can remember some people having a 24-hour bug, including me, but that is all I can remember. Besides, if we were sick, we would still get up in the morning and be ready to hump. In the bush there wasn't a sick call.

And speaking of pills and being sick, I have read in other books about grunts intentionally not taking their malaria pills, hoping to get an early trip home. We didn't have those either, but again, we never got sick.

The monsoon season was also part mental and part physical. It was primarily physical, enduring the season, but the mental portion did go hand in hand with it. You also have to recognize that I am trying to individualize the different characteristics or factors of being hardcore, but you have to keep in mind that all these factors are mixed together and not separated in a combat zone.

Since I am overlapping physical and mental factors, the next item is not a trait or a defining factor to the definition of hardcore. I believe the next subject is a byproduct of the hardcore person or personality. A person needs to be hardcore for the next item: The SKULLS or in particular "the skull". After a few weeks in the Recon platoon, we were in the rear for a standdown. Most likely, it was Thanksgiving. There was a skull in the clubhouse that had been there for unknown months, and it was a ritual of the Recon man to drink out of the skull. As a recent newcomer to the platoon, I took my turn pouring a Coke in the skull and chugging it empty. A little gross, but it indicated a state of mind. Besides, the skull had so much alcohol ran through it that it was probably sterile.

Doc McGuire drinking out of the older Skull. Notice Sgt. Delong unaffected
by the event.

This is the skull that we found, and "Four Eyes". The hat, M-16, and jungle shirt are the author's. Notice the dying vegetation from defoliants.

But that was not "the skull". During a mission in an area that had been sprayed with Agent Orange, we came across a shallow grave marked by the leg bones. Being it was a common Vietnamese practice to bury weapons in gravesites or make a weapons cache look like a gravesite, it was decided to dig up the area and investigate. Besides, isn't that defined as "recon"? I can remember the area well. The stench of death and decaying foliage is something you don't forget, no matter how hard you try. The area looked like death. Instead of green jungle, it was dying brown. When we first came across the grave, several of us had walked over it before we realized what it was.

As I was eating my L.R.R. P. ration that night, I kept noticing a rotting smell that would not go away. Eventually, I realized it was decaying human flesh on my boots. Apparently, I had picked it up when crossing over the grave. I took my bayonet, scraped it off my boot and continued eating.

Later that day one of the teams opened the grave only to find some bones and a skull. Since we were young troops with an ego we decided we needed a skull of our own to drink out of. It was brought back and because of the radio conversation in which I told them to bring it back, it was given to me to carry. So I cleaned it up that night, removed the remaining brain matter and hair and a few teeth, and placed it on the back of my ruck. I humped it for a couple of weeks in the bush. I imagine that would have been quite a sight to see, a skull bouncing on the back of a ruck. I believe "Water Buffalo" was going in for an R&R and he took it down to a stream to rinse it off, and then took it to the rear. "Wild Bill" was positive we cleaned it in the mess hall upon our return to the rear but I do not remember the instance. Anyway, as I was the one that humped it in the bush for a couple of weeks, it seemed appropriate that I would initiate it in the Recon tradition. I poured my Coke into the skull (it held 12 ounces) and tipped it back. As I was drinking my Coke out of this skull, some of the fluid was leaking through the sutures and running down my throat. This obviously added to the sensation. The skull was then passed around to other old timers to initiate it with beer. Some of the newer Recon guys passed on drinking out of the skull. I somewhat felt this was a ritual of passage into the state of "hardcore". Apparently, they were not hardcore enough at that point in time. I will also admit that the taste of a Coke drank out of a fresh skull is not especially pleasing or one to experience on a regular basis.

I understand the "drinking out of the skull ritual" became a source for starting a fight or two, as "Wild Bill" reminded me. We were on a rare standdown in Camp Eagle and had assumed our reserved front row seats at the battalion theater area. Apparently I started off the ritual of "chugging from the skull" by pouring a Coke into the skull, chugging it down, and passing it on. The skull was passed on to the next Recon man to pour in a beer, chug, and pass on. After several 12-ounce cans of beverage had been emptied into the skull, the entertainer realized what we were doing and stopped the show, then left the stage. This obviously aggravated the other troops watching the show, and a fight followed. Maybe this was why we were typically isolated from other Line Companies.

If you noticed, it was mentioned that we had reserved front row seats in the theater area. This was another hint we were different. The officers sat behind us as well as everyone else.

Also, only Recon drank from the skull. This was a ritual that others did not participate in. Nor did Recon typically associate with troops in Line Companies.

You need to understand at this point that drinking out of the skull was not being disrespectful to the dead. It was something we did due to our state of mind. This is part of the reason this book was written, so people can try to have a limited understanding of how we thought, and where our state of mind was, or wasn't. It is also partially the insanity of being in a war. I am not trying to paint a morbid picture or gross people out and make them sick. I am trying to tell the facts of how the conflict we were in changed us.

Another factor that combines physical and mental conditions is the time we spent in the field. In the 1966-1967 era, the Recon platoon was part of Headquarters Company. They had three very large teams composed from two platoons. Each would rotate, a week in the field and two weeks out. Normally, they knew the area, and looked for signs of change or movement all through the area. Many Line Companies during our era were similar. Often times, they would go to a firebase instead of the base camp, but they were able to get out of the bush and let down. We were normally in places where we were the only American troops operating, and it was unusual for us to be in familiar territory. The majority of the time, the only trails we saw were those regularly used by the North Vietnamese. Normally, we were in their backyard.

We had about three or four days out of the field during Thanksgiving, and ten or eleven days out during Christmas. We left on December 31, 1970, and it was over ninety-three (93) days before we came in. This included the height of the monsoons and cold weather. I have yet to talk to anyone whose unit spent that much consecutive time in the bush. From December 31, 1970, through part of June 1971, we had seven (7) days out of the bush. Most of us were out another seven for R&R. Figuring from when I got into the Recon platoon, that equates to approximately 7 ½ months, with approximately 27 days (give or take a couple) out of the bush. We didn't even get to stand down after Co Pung!

I should also mention personal hygiene, and clarify "getting cleaned up". In my old letters that were sent home, I mentioned to my sister, in a letter dated January of 1971, about having a real shower. Normally, when near a stream or in the 'soons we would take a towel, or whatever, and try to remove some jungle from us, without soap. Soap would leave aromas or fragrances that we could be tracked by. Often times, the water wasn't very clean but we would go through the motions. During the 'soons the water was cold so we couldn't hop in and take a bath. It was just an attempt to get some crud off.

In the letter, I told her that I had a real shower in November when we were out of the bush. And that was the only one I had in November! Then I proceeded to write that I also had a shower in December during the Christmas standdown. So far, that adds up to two showers in two months. The month of January came and went with no shower. February also came and went without a shower. Can you imagine the odor we had! March also came and went without a shower. It wasn't until I came in for my R&R in the first week of April that I showered. The rest of Recon came in three or four days later. Not bad, three whole showers in 5 months! I had more showers than that on my first day in Bangkok.

In the time frame I was in the Recon platoon, we spent more time in the field than most grunts with two consecutive one-year tours in Vietnam. We could never let down and unwind like the majority of grunts because we didn't come out of the jungle. Yes, we moved from place to place via combat assaults, but those were not picnics, and even more stressful than humping.

I believe a problem we had for morale was similar to what we call "cabin fever" today. We were left in the bush for so long that we got "jungle fever". That is, we were "cooped up" in the jungle for so long that it had to affect our state of mind. Being hardcore, as a lot of people will tell you they are (and they probably are), is one thing, but adding the factor of being cooped up in the jungle for so long added to the animalistic attitude we had. Most combat soldiers had a chance to unwind or let down on a regular basis, we didn't. I think that we had so much stress compressed into us, from being in an extended defensive mode in the field and enduring combat assaults, that all of us mentally changed forever. This was not a situation that would allow us to revert back to being normal in two or three years or even twenty or thirty years, or ever!

A reasonable analogy of this is being in a car wreck when you were young; you broke a leg and, thirty years later, still walk with a limp. The accident was thirty years ago but you still limp as a result of it. You also never forget why you limp. Every step you take in some form reminds you of your accident. I still "limp" because I am hardcore from a "wreck" thirty years ago. Just because you are removed from a situation doesn't mean the problem goes away.

Being in the bush for such extended periods of time created problems that follow us today. I still stop when I am in the woods when I see something flicker or move. I do not expect to see a V.C. or N.V.A. pop out from behind a tree, but it is almost an instinctive reaction to stop and check out what is moving.

I was talking to a 'Nam vet one day and we were reminiscing about our days in the bush. This particular individual is a recovered alcoholic. We discussed life in the bush, and eventually his past drinking problems were aired out. An interesting analogy of hardcore came up. One of the reasons he drank so heavily was because he didn't want to face the world sober. He needed his bottle. Sometimes I look at losing my hardcore mentality as "sobering" up.

In 'Nam we needed to be hardcore to survive. In today's world I don't think I would want to lose my hardcore defenses. I have always said that it gave me a "warm and fuzzy" feeling, so I have the ability to cope with anything that is thrown at me. I don't think I want to face the world as the majority of the people do. The hardcore mentality takes away a lot of the pain, stress, and grief that most people have to endure. While I'll be the first to admit that today I am still too mentally hardcore, I think that I always want to carry a strong percentage of it instead of "sobering" up.

There are other advantages of being hardcore that helped us survive in 'Nam. When you are hardcore, you lose emotion as a way to cope. Seeing people die or injured gives little feeling because the emotion is gone. Look into the eyes of a hardcore vet and try to find emotion. Except for an occasional tear for a lost friend, the eyes are empty. The lack of emotion allows you to think clearer. Decisions are based upon facts when the emotions are gone. I think it helped us to survive because we could make decisions based upon facts. Later in the book, I mention being kicked out of the field. All the events and decisions we made were on the spot and were correct, because we were hardcore and had no emotion in making the decisions we did.

Many people will tell you that they have become hard or hardened through the years. Undoubtedly they are accurate in their statement, but it is also based upon society's standard of being hardened. As stated, they have become hardened "through the years". It may have taken them 20, 30, or 40 years to become hardened. Looking at my close friends "Four Eyes", "Wild Bill" and myself, the three of us were listed as killed in action together twice. We had over 50 combat assaults apiece, spent excessive time in the jungle, became extremely hardcore, and survived the 'soons. I was Platoon Sergeant and Platoon Leader of an extremely elite unit, and three weeks after returning home I reached the ripe old age of 22. "Wild Bill" and "Four Eyes" are younger than I am. Our hardening was similar to that of heat-treating metals. We went through extreme changes very quickly to become hardened and we will stay that way for life.

Another thing that needs to be stressed about being hardcore is, it is like an addiction; it controls us, we do not control it. It is worse than a person with an alcohol problem. No matter how hard we try, the hardcore state of mind is very much in control and extremely dominant. It may not be obvious to the untrained eye but it is very much in control of our emotions.

Being on the defensive is another symptom. Even in the rear, we were on defense. Today is no different. As I walk down a street I watch every person, look down every alley or dark corner, and start thinking about routes of escape or defense. Many of us, including me, cannot sit in a restaurant with our backs to the door. Defensively we must be able to see who is coming and going. Instead of being defensive, today we are considered extremely hyper-vigilant. We are still watching our backs.

SLEEPING AND SLEEPING WITH ONE EYE OPEN

Probably everyone reading this has experienced sleeping with one eye open at some point in your life, for a limited time, regardless of age. If you are a youngster, or remember being a child, you may have been afraid of sleeping in the dark or on occasions heard noises that kept you awake. You may have thought that something or someone was in your closet or under your bed. Any noise and you would startle and wake up, or maybe you thought you saw a shadow move.

Another good example of sleeping with one eye open is the new parent. Every time the new baby sniffles or coughs you jump up to make sure they are okay. Now let's expand upon that thought for a minute. Suppose your new baby is sick and running a fever. With every whimper you are normally checking in on the infant and you check in every half-hour to hour just to make sure. You are hoping the infant will be okay and thinking about how precious their life is. You are sleeping in a twilight sleep. You don't remember falling asleep or waking up. You know you haven't slept, yet the clock shows a different hour every time you look at it.

You also have to get up in the morning and go to work. It is a cold rainy day and you forgot your raincoat at work, and the only place to park is several blocks away from work. You are tired and wanting to sleep, but you know you can't. Then you remember that when you get to work you have all those heavy boxes to move around all day long. After a few days of this, you start feeling like a zombie. You haven't had a good night's sleep in days. Up and down all night long. Listening to every noise coming out of the crib. You are starting to be cranky and irritable, craving for some one to relieve you. Now let's expand this thought into weeks. Now, how do you feel? Past the state of being a zombie? These are some examples of sleeping with one eye open and how you feel during this time frame. We have all done it at some point in our lives. But the descriptions previously listed are a milder version of what we did. At least you were sleeping on a bed or couch, and it was warm and dry.

This is a limited explanation of what we dealt with, except our situation went on for weeks or months at times. Regardless of what happened, we would get up in the morning, pack up the ruck and prepare for another hump in the jungle. Some of the scenarios I mentioned previously that the average person has experienced, bear some resemblance to how we felt mentally. I say "some resemblance" because the comparisons are limited to being tired and knowing that any little noise will wake you up. I think that is about the only common point though.

In the real life experiences of the average person, you do not have to contend with carrying 60% or more of your body weight on your back. Nor also contend with the possibilities of being ambushed, finding booby traps, going on combat assaults, or being in a firefight at any point in time.

Now think about how you would feel if you have slept with one eye open for several days or weeks, and on your way to work a car pulls out in front of you, and you slide all over the road in an attempt to miss them. After you have said a few choice words you recompose yourself, try to get your heart out of your throat, and go on. After a few moments you realize that your mind is in a haze. You are very tired and you are also carrying a high from the adrenaline rush from the car pulling out in front of you. This is the closest I can come to describing how we felt after any close call. Whether it was a noise, shadow, a combat assault, possible booby trap or any kind of movement.

At this point, I need to describe what we slept on and under; or our version of a bed. A poncho, or if we set up with someone, two ponchos, a poncho liner, and that was it! We would set up the ponchos about waist high. Just high enough to possibly eat under during the 'soons but also low enough that they were not higher than the vegetation around us. The spot we picked was near a small tree or bush, so we tied the center of the poncho up and found something to stretch the corners to. That would leave a little over half of our bodies on the second poncho, with the rest on the ground, mud, or whatever. Sitting up near trees also meant tree roots to contend with. As we attempted to sleep at night, we had to get as comfortable as possible between the roots.

The author at the NDP with equipment, poncho liner, and poncho. Hooch is at top of picture.

My pillow was my spare battery, and I would take my shirt off and lay it on top of the battery, and sleep in my nightshirt. To get warm in the 'soons, Gary and I would double up our poncho liners and sleep back to back with the radio placed between our heads, as we had to report a "negative sit rep" every hour, every night.

Good sleep in the bush was a precious thing. A good night's sleep was rare, if it ever occurred, because of sleeping with one eye open. Today it is referred to as being hyper-vigilant. All through this book I have referenced our status as being on the defensive. Regardless of what was occurring, we were on the defensive. Eating, playing cards, brushing our teeth, drinking water, cleaning an M-16, whispering, humping the bush, whatever you name, we were ready for action. Why would sleep be any different? It is somewhat like reading a book and deciding not to blink your eyes; you can't do it! Sleep was no different. We all closed our eyes and had grenades or our M-16 beside us or between our legs, ready to go to "rock and roll" in a blink.

The mindset was to listen and be ready as we closed our eyes for a rest. I rarely remember true sleep in the bush. We were somewhat in a twilight sleep. We were aware of what was going on, but not truly awake, or asleep.

Often times when the watch was being passed, which meant it was your turn to stay awake, watch and listen, while the others were resting. You would not have to wake the next guy up. He would awaken by your movement or by what little noise you made getting to the spot where he was sleeping.

As you consider these conditions, also remember the other factors of being tired. From carrying around the ruck, being tired from humping for three hours, you were still wet, you were cold, and rank smelling from not having bathed in a month. Our clothes were dirty and ripped, and we were unable to sleep soundly. This situation went on for weeks on end. Sometimes when we moved we thought, or assumed we were being followed, and sometimes we heard movement in the bush. Maybe we were being probed or maybe it was just an animal, but regardless of what it was, the depth or quality of sleep was even less than previously.

During the summer months, when there was a full moon, the terrain had an eerie effect. We could walk from hooch to hooch and see everything in between. This made sleep difficult because our eyes would play tricks on us. We would swear that we saw something move. And maybe we did, a branch or bush waving in the breeze, but regardless, something moved and it tripped the instinct of sleeping with one eye open.

I can remember situations when we heard movement of some form and we called for illumination rounds to light up the area. Illumination rounds were basically flares on small parachutes. When fired, they slowly fell to the earth, doing a reasonable job of lighting up the area. Unfortunately, the shadows created by these were very similar to the full moon effect, and no matter how tired we were, the mind didn't allow us to sleep because we were on a higher level of defense.

We had an opposite situation during the monsoons: total pitch-black darkness. When one could not see his hand in front of his face, it was extremely hard to get over to the next man for watch. During the monsoons with the cloud cover, no moon, fog, and dense jungle, the darkness was darker than dark. I have heard many joking comments about not being able to see your hand in front of your face, but in this case it was no joke, it was very real.

I remember a situation when we were on a steep hillside during the monsoons. I believe we were in team size units. My hour of watch was from 2 a.m. to 3 a.m. My time was up and the next guy to awaken was probably less than fifteen feet away. All I had to do was walk around a bush and pass the watch. I had the option of going around the top of the bush, but I opted not to take that route because if I slipped, I would fall into the bush and possibly give our position away or scare the hell out of everyone. I opted to walk in front of the bush, and sure enough I slid. Being as it was pitch-black, it was hard to tell up from down and left from right.

After I had walked further than I should have, I knew I had a problem. I couldn't make any noise out of fear of awakening the others and being fired upon. I took several more steps, trying to find my way back, when I felt something taut along the path. It was our trip flare that had a claymore mine behind it, and I was on the wrong side! One mistake and I was dead meat! Once my heart started to beat again, I knew where I was. I carefully stepped over the trip wire and made my way up the path to the hooch I was hunting for. I don't remember whom I woke up, but when he looked at the time and realized most of his watch was over (it was 3:46 a.m.), he whispered asking me if I had fallen asleep. I responded that I couldn't sleep so I pulled part of his watch for him. I walked back to my hooch by going around the top of the bush, covered up, and trembled the rest of the night (or morning as it were).

Another thing you did not do was to shake someone's feet to wake them up. The immediate mental impression was that the enemy was crawling over them to slit their throat. Even today, it is a mistake to awaken many 'Nam veterans by shaking or touching their feet.

When I returned home from 'Nam, I lived at my mother's house for a short time, and she was scared to be in the room to wake me up. It was always a shout from downstairs to wake me up. Because of the sleeping patterns and defenses we developed, shaking or climbing across a vet getting into bed can be a mistake.

The few times we went to the rear we normally slept well. Usually, we received incoming rounds when we returned to the rear because the V.C. heard we were returning (that was the only time they could find us), but the sleep there was better. We were dry, and slept on a very comfortable cot (compared to the ground), or a very soft wooden floor. After sleeping on the ground between tree roots and whatever, it is amazing how comfortable a wood floor can be. I think we even slept with both eyes shut!

Later in the book, I discuss defense and how it affects us today. Sleeping with one eye open is still a problem for me today and a common problem for many 'Nam vets. It varies because of each person's make up and the experiences they had. The more traumatic the events, the harder it is to sleep with both eyes shut.

This also ties in with flashbacks and bad dreams. We often relive past events of firefights, assaults, and other horrors of war lurking in the dark corners of our minds, and we cannot let go of them. When this happens on a frequent basis, we are reluctant to go to sleep and often times fight sleep. Afraid of waking up and wondering if we are still in 'Nam, or even alive.

CHANGE

As I write this, the word <u>change</u> becomes one of the keys to understanding the problems and dilemmas of 'Nam vets. Yes, we did change, but we did not go there intending to drink out of human skulls like it was a root beer mug, nor did we intend on becoming hardcore and being forced to contend with the problems of being hardcore. We did not intend on becoming cold and emotionless. Look in our eyes, the eyes tell it all! Change occurred as we entered conflicts, firefights, combat assaults, the environment, stress, and being away from home.

Part of understanding the changes we went through, is told by the eyes. I have stated many times that the eyes tell it all. The faraway stare is a major part of understanding change. For me to handle or deal with the situation, part of me was left behind. I went there whole, but when I returned, there was less of me than before. I lost a part of myself that was taken for granted. Often times I didn't realize I even had it. It could be called emotion, but that is only part of it. It was partially my soul or inner self. It was the part of me that allows me to jump with joy and have eyes that gleam. That part was left behind. Not because I wanted to leave it behind but because it was scattered behind me, bit by bit, with every combat assault, every firefight, every time I slept with one eye open, every hump, every time I drank out of a skull, every time I wondered if I was about to take my last breath. It was slowly extracted from me and left a void that will not be filled!

I did not know that I was going to be on combat assaults, nor did I know that I was going to sleep in the mud, nor did I know I was going to carry a hundred pound ruck, nor did I even know that I would be cold in Vietnam. Nor did I know I was going to be in an elite unit. Nor did I know that mentally, I would never come out of the jungle. There are many things I didn't know about in preparation to go to 'Nam. And even if I had, the tasks that we faced were more overwhelming than we could have prepared for.

Many of these changes were major, but some were minor. The major changes will affect us till the day we take our last breath. We may not always like the change we made nor do we always control them, but whether we like it or not, they affect our everyday lives and actions.

I don't like the fact that my ears ring from being on too many assaults, but I can't control it. I don't like the fact that I am always on the defensive, but it is an automatic mechanism (are your eyes blinking?) that I don't control. I don't necessarily like being emotionless, but it is part of a protective mechanism. Being hardcore- sometimes I like it, and sometimes I don't, but it has a mind of its own. I didn't plan on these things happening, nor did anyone else, but these are the outgrowths of war and out of our control.

Odds are that after reading this book, you will also change. It may be minor or major, but you will change in some form. You may change your understanding of 'Nam vets, or you may realize that we didn't want to change. Possibly you will change the way you converse with other people and notice the story the eyes are telling you. Or maybe you will change your perspective of life and simply appreciate being able to go to bed at night in a dry bed with dry clothes on and wake up dry. When you started reading this book, you did not plan on changing, but you will have changed in some form when you are done. Whether minor or major, good or bad, you will have changed. You are no different from us, because we didn't plan to change either. There are many reasons that caused us to change. Change was a necessity to survive, but people have to understand that change was not necessarily our idea. It evolved from the environment of conflict.

All of us are involved with change based upon our everyday life, our jobs, family, and friends. Change is a fact of life. The level of change is directly proportional to the level of severity or challenge you encounter.

It is not much different than your son or daughter going off to college, and after a year, you tell them how much they have changed. We went off to a different college and majored in survival and jungle warfare, with real life and death situations. It's not much different in concept, except the fact that the level of intensity and stress was on a tremendously different scale. The severity was more intense and profound.

As you read all the different perspectives of the environment, physical challenges, mental stress, combat assaults, being in the jungle for extended periods, being shot at, and not knowing if you would live to the next hour, take a moment and ask yourself a simple question. Would I not change? If you answer yes, then you are being truthful to yourself and have some understanding of how we are. If your answer is no, then you are only fooling yourself.

Another portion of change that we often forget about, is the year of our life that we skipped in the "world". Other people in our age group, that didn't go to 'Nam, were able to keep in touch with daily events around the world, we couldn't. Think about when you go on vacation for a week or two and have to catch up on the newspapers for all the news. It takes a couple days to settle down, but you have had the radio to listen to and keep abreast of current events.

When I came home it was like I had hit a time warp. I would ask questions about certain people only to find they had moved, or married, or died, or whatever, but we were totally unaware of the world changing around us because we were basically cut off from the outside world. Yes, we did receive the "Stars and Stripes" newspaper but being it was military, it was obviously "cleansed" before it was printed. We might have known who won the World Series two months after it was over, but to pick up a telephone to catch up on the latest events didn't happen. You cannot imagine the feeling of walking down the street in your hometown and being a stranger that is out of touch with the times.

Another event that happened several times, was to be visiting with some friends and have the radio on. As you are conversing, a song comes on and it's the first time you have heard it. You like the song and think you might hear it later in the day, but when it is over the DJ announces "it was popular one year ago today". And you think, where was I? Oh, now I know why I don't remember that song.

The whole world changed around us as well. We had many facets of change to deal with besides the war. Our families and friends changed and we had a lot of catching up to do. When you are having a conversation with some friends one day, sit back for a moment and think of all the things that have happened around you in the last year. Now try to have that conversation with them but not discuss any of those events from the past year. It doesn't take long to realize that you are feeling out of place and have nothing to say. That is pretty much how I felt!

Change is something we all deal with on a regular basis. Whether it is related to having children, not having children, getting a new car, changing jobs, losing a parent or loved one, being divorced, trying a new restaurant, or a thousand other things. We all face change, or the results of change, on a daily basis.

We, the Viet Nam vets, are facing the results of change on a daily basis, and hopefully the readers of this book can realize it. As we deal with today's environment, we react with the tools that kept us alive during the high tension and stressful environment of 'Nam. So many times people think we are crazy for reacting the way we do, but it is basically an instinct.

A good analogy for the reader comparing change is this. Convince yourself that you will not blink your eyes while reading the rest of this book. You can't do it, can you! It is automatic to blink, it is automatic for me to act and be defensive! No matter how hard I try or want to change certain aspects of my thinking, it can't be done. They can be modified or softened, as time erodes the memories, but the basic pattern is still there. Sometimes, something that trips a mental trigger will also set you back. I believe the correct term is "reverting". Reverting is when the mind takes over, with or without your conscious approval, and defense mechanisms take over.

There is a saying I have used for a long period of time. This is probably the most appropriate place in the book for it. Consider the comments referring to being hardcore, the eyes tell it all, sleeping with one eye open, change, humping, the monsoons and the summer heat, and all the other insanities of war. Many people think we (the 'Nam vets) are crazy. My definition or opinion of sanity and insanity is this:

> *There is a fine line between sanity and insanity.*
> *Sanity is being crazy and knowing how to deal with it.*
> *Insanity is when you are not dealing with it.*

I know I am dealing with my insanities and craziness. You have to ask yourself if you are dealing with your craziness properly, before you can judge us. And in most cases, the average person crosses that fine line on a regular basis before they adequately deal with their problems or the insanities of life. So, where do you fit into my definition?

BEING DEFENSIVE

I should also discuss being defensive, as it is an outgrowth of change, being hardcore, and a multitude of events listed earlier. Most people think of defense as someone on a football team or basketball team. The defensive team or player's function is to prevent the opposition from "scoring". They position themselves to reduce the passing lane, or have an easy shot, or whatever the scoring method is.

In 'Nam we were also on a team. We didn't play sports but our mission was to prevent the opposition from "scoring" on us. That is to say, kill us. Being defensive, for a combat veteran, is automatic. Our defensive strategy was a simple one. Don't be seen and don't be heard. Many events mentioned in this book so far, refer to being on defense. There are many facets to the definition of defense. Whispering, being overly alert (hyper-vigilant), sleeping with one eye open, spacing when humping, just to name a few. Today, we are still on defense.

The next time you talk to a 'Nam vet, look into his eyes and notice that faraway look. Typically, as you are talking to him and looking in his eyes, you will see his eyes roaming or darting about the room. He may be trying to locate the exits or see who is behind him, if he is not already sitting in the corner. When someone walks by, odds are he is evaluating whether that person is a threat to him, or he will lift his head and notice the individual or make eye contact with the person. He is on the defensive for his safety. It is ingrained in his brain. He knows that for him to survive he has to be on defense, even today. It is still part of his survival mechanism.

Doc McGuire getting ready to go on patrol.

Howard "Pappy" Grabill and captured N.V.A. weapon.

It is very common for 'Nam combat vets to avoid crowds because it is too hard to watch everyone. We walk in areas that are less crowded because we feel more secure there. But, as we walk, we are constantly looking about to see what is occurring around us. If you ever have the occasion to walk with the combat vet, notice the anticipation of his movements. Constantly looking about, maybe partially relaxed because they are with a "friendly" but still on edge. But also notice his reaction if a bird suddenly flies by or something moves in the bushes. It is a motion of defense. He probably won't duck or hit the ground, but he will notice the slightest movements. A simple piece of paper snagged in a bush will annoy him because it is constantly grabbing his attention by simply moving in the breeze.

Many 'Nam vets will walk the "perimeter" before going to bed at nights. The routine is as varied as the individual and his experiences, but the common denominator is being on defense. They have to make the last security check to make sure things will be ok. It may be as simple as making sure all the doors are locked and then double-checking them again. Some vets cannot sleep unless their bedroom door is locked or chained securely. Some vets, because of past events, cannot go to sleep until they have walked the perimeter of their property. Some do this while carrying a weapon. It is the only way they can have peace of mind to sleep. Most wives of vets know that they must go to bed at the same time or before their husband, and the vast majority also know that they do not crawl over their husband getting into bed, or touch his feet. It was, and still is, part of his defense mechanism.

Some youngsters cannot sleep without their teddy bear, doll, or a particular blanket. It is a sense of security for them. For 'Nam vets, it is a similar mindset but on a much deeper level.

Everything Recon did in 'Nam was primarily defensive. After months on end of being defensive for 24 hours a day, 7 days a week, you cannot avoid being defensive.

Many 'Nam vets also carry weapons or cannot sleep unless there is a loaded weapon close by. The intent is not to lie in bed waiting to shoot someone, but it is part of the defense mechanism. How did we sleep in 'Nam? With a weapon by our side. It is part of what kept us alive. Today, it is often the same mindset. It is part of what keeps us alive. It allows us to be in a defensive mode in case something happens. If we need a weapon, it is there. We are ready.

By the way, why do you carry a spare tire for your car? Aren't you being defensive in case you need it? Do you carry a spare tire hoping to use it? I doubt it. Both you and we (the 'Nam vets) hope and pray that we never need our "spare tires", but if ever needed, we have them. It is part of our defensive mechanisms. Our levels are on a different plane but we have similar perspectives.

When you drive defensively you are trying to anticipate what the driver, ahead or behind you, is going to do. We are no different. We are not driving defensively. We are living defensively. As you are driving and someone pulls out in front of you, reactions tell you to swerve or hit the brakes. The last time it happened to you, did you pause and think, "Oh gee, maybe I should slow down?" Of course you didn't! Before you could bat an eyelash you had hit the brakes or swerved to miss what was ahead of you.

We live with the same mindset for defense. We don't think about when it is time to put on the "brakes" as we approach a situation, but we instinctively "swerve" to avoid oncoming people obstacles.

It is probably easier for you to NOT hit the brakes the next time someone pulls out in front of you, than it is for us to hit the brakes on being defensive.

COMBAT ASSAULTS

A combat assault, or a "C.A." as we referred to them, is probably the most stressful and mentally draining thing we could have experienced, or did experience. It is probably the most complicated ingredient of the hardcore formula to define in detail because the emotional stresses, the highs and lows, and levels of excitement and anticipation are unreal. Not only that, there is really not any accurate way to describe the mental effects of an assault. The only way to fully understand it is to experience one, and I wouldn't recommend it to anyone.

As you read this, think of the last time you were driving on snow and ice and approached a long steep hill. As you start to descend the hill, a semi is jackknifed at the bottom and the driver is standing next to the truck, waving at you, trying to get your attention. As you hit the brakes the car starts to slide down the hill on the ice and you spin sideways. You are starting to lose control of your vehicle. You are wondering if you will be able to stop. You think about trying to slide into the ditch or hitting another car. Will the driver get out of the way fast enough? Your brain is running a hundred miles an hour. It seems like everything is slow motion as you try to assess the situation and miss the truck and driver. Everything around you seems to be out of control. Your heart is pounding faster and faster, your adrenaline is pumping like crazy and the palms of your hands are sweaty. You look around to see if there are any other cars or trucks. Then, you finally stop inches from the truck!

You take a deep breath, lay your head on the steering wheel for a few brief moments, mumble a few words of relief, and go on. A couple of blocks down the road you suddenly realize that you could have been killed if you had hit the truck. You then realize that your fingers are still clamped on the steering wheel. And you then notice that your palms are still sweaty, the heart has slowed down some but is still beating rapidly. The adrenaline rush is still in effect, and you realize that not only are your palms sweaty, you are perspiring all over. You then think about your spouse, children, and loved ones. Twenty minutes later you arrive home and get out of your car. Then you realize your knees are weak and your legs hurt from being tensed up so tight during the near miss. You notice that your shirt is damp from all the perspiration. You walk into the house, sit down, and realize how you almost "bit the dust". If you have ever been in a close call similar to this then you understand part of the assault trauma and terror. The whole accident scenario, from the time the car started sliding on the hill till you stopped, took a few seconds; maybe 6 or 7 seconds; maybe 10 seconds at the most.

Going in on a combat assault has some similar emotions, except the assault is planned. There is plenty of time to think about what is going to happen. Many things pass through your mind as you are waiting. The heart pumping and the adrenaline rush last into the tens of minutes or possibly even close to an hour in the assault. The car wreck scenario lasted seconds.

On the slick as we were getting ready to go in, there was plenty of time for us to ponder whether this was going to be our last assault and how bad it was going to be. We had several minutes to ponder upcoming events. The near miss was only seconds.

Another big difference is, when you stopped in the near miss you could take a deep breath, compose yourself, and go on. In the assault, after you hit the ground, you continue on. No time to let down and recompose yourself. In the wreck scenario, no one is shooting at you. That increases the intensity ten fold. And this portion of the description is only comparing a part of the assault.

To begin with, a combat assault is simply defined as getting on a helicopter and being deposited in another location. But, that is being simply stated.

First, all our assaults started by being extracted from the landing zone we occupied. Whether it was for a couple of days during the monsoons, or we had been there for 15 minutes, we had to have it secured.

As you are visualizing the description of the extraction, go back to the near miss scenario and put yourself in place of the truck driver. His feeling as he is wondering whether you are going to miss him or not, is the closest thing I can think of in describing the emotion felt during the extraction. It is not the same situation but it will help put you in the right frame of mind.

The next event involved everyone taking up a defensive position because the choppers were coming in. At this point, the choppers and we were very vulnerable. Also remember that half of the time there were only eight or ten of us on the ground, securing the L.Z. Not exactly an overwhelming number of people on our side. In the best cases, it was maybe twenty to twenty four of us.

Upon hearing the choppers, radio contact was made and four words were uttered that still make the hair on the back of my neck stand up; "in bound; pop smoke", which means we were preparing to tell everyone where we were. In Recon, where the goal of survival hinges upon being undetectable (or in today's terminology, being stealthy), popping smoke went against our grain. We would receive confirmation from the pilot as to the color of the smoke. This was due to the fact that Viet Cong and North Vietnamese would also pop smoke to lure the pilots into their gun sights.

Goofy grape, mellow yellow, or banana were common responses. Red smoke was only popped if we would be receiving fire after the initial smoke was popped or if we were already receiving fire.

The only good news here is, when we traveled we always had a red team with us. A red team is a pair of Cobra gunships that could release more hell than I would ever want to face. The Cobras or "snakes", as they were referred to, were a great deterrent as well as some peace of mind for us.

You also have to realize part of the trauma or mental stress we were dealing with was due to being taken out of our element, somewhat like a fish out of water. Because of our experience and experiences, Recon men felt safer in the jungle because we were in our element or a place we could disappear into and defend. In a slick, we were sitting ducks. The N.V.A. could hear the slicks coming for miles, just as we could, so they would be ready for us. The whole process was opposite of what we were best at.

When we were in small teams it took two helicopters to extract us. It usually took only four helicopters to remove the whole platoon. On rare occasions, it would take five slicks to move us. The extraction was always a precarious event. We were at our most vulnerable position because, as the slicks came in, we had to move as quickly as possible to the bird and get on while maintaining a defensive posture. All of this happened while carrying a 100 to 120-pound ruck. Remember all the comments earlier about the ruck? Here it is, like a boat anchor. Ever run with a 120-pound boat anchor?

There was the anxiety of waiting on the slicks, giving away our position, hoping no one is shooting at us, running with the ruck, our heart in our throats, and falling into the bird. Then we were okay. Almost. Next we had to get some altitude to make sure we were high enough to be out of range of small arms fire.

Then we were okay for a while; most of Viet Nam is a beautiful country from the air. The green jungles, mountains and rivers, from our vantagepoint, were quite a site.

A typical view of our position on a slick and the view we had going in on the assault.

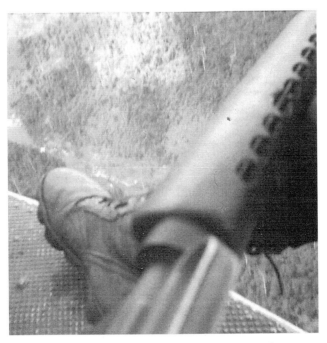

Another example of how we sat on the slicks.

Our vantagepoint would also not pass OSHA standards. We would get into the slick rucks first. Our feet would be dangling down and we could see everything around us. There were no seats or straps to hold us in, just flat, empty floor. We would be sitting on the helicopter like a chair with no back. The weight of our ruck helped to hold us back, but our feet and legs were just hanging there. We would now be a few thousand feet in the air and just sitting there.

Once we were airborne the ride became interesting. We had a wonderful view of the complete area. If it was during the summer months, the props forcing the air down on us would cool us off. If it was during the monsoons, we got wetter.

I can remember, on two or three occasions, when the man next to me sat his ruck on my hand as he entered, never intentionally, mind you, but because of the awkwardness of trying to enter a bird ruck first. It was not a graceful move. But regardless, it would hurt for a while and sometimes bruise, but being as we were concerned about upcoming events, it didn't matter much.

For a quick recap; an adrenaline rush that would bring us up for several hours, lots of excitement, an enjoyable view (normally) and a little discomfort. What was next? The ride got wild!

Before the description of the insertion, I should state my location during the extraction, ride and insertion. Being as I was the platoon R.T.O., I was always on the first bird out and first bird in. Today I question my thinking, but at the time it all made perfectly good sense. The "first bird in" or "the duck hunting" theory, was that, when someone was shooting at us, normally they did not have their lead-in adjusted till three or four birds later. By this time we were on the ground and ready for the next events. Also, it was known that the enemy would normally let the first bird or two land because they knew Americans didn't want to leave a few men on the ground alone. Sounded like a good theory at the time, and still doesn't sound too bad.

The terror of the insertion is even harder to describe. My mind would be racing one hundred miles an hour. I would have had several minutes or longer to anticipate the events that were about to unfold. My mind would be reeling from going through all the different scenarios of the insertion. Would it be hot or cold? What was the cover like? What about booby traps? We would still be on an adrenaline rush from being extracted; we would be trying to position ourselves and the rucks so we could, somewhat gracefully, fall out the slick when we came close to the ground. We would be checking our M-16s to make sure we were ready to "rock and roll" if necessary, while still wondering if this would be a "hot" L.Z. where someone would try to kill us (again). My heart would have moved back up into my throat as I took a deep breath and

I would have cherished it because I knew it might be the last breath I would ever take.

Then all hell broke loose. Those magnificent snakes with us then lined up and cut loose with everything they had. The whoosh of the rockets always broke the trance of thought first. Occasionally, we would hear the rockets cut loose, but never hear any explosions. Those were my favorites because they were the flechette rounds. Thousands of little nail-like darts ripping to shreds anything that stood or was standing in front of them. Then the 40-m.m. cannon or mini guns let loose. There wasn't a sound more heartwarming to hear on an assault than the deep roar of the mini guns. They could lay down so much lead that we were glad they were on our side. After both snakes prepped or "softened" the L.Z., it was "show time".

"Show time" was when things really got exciting. As the birds were coming close to the L.Z., the door gunners would open up with their M-60's to level anything coming at us. It was an attempt to keep the enemy's head down so we could get on the ground and they could get off the ground.

We positioned ourselves to offload rapidly, so when the bird was close to the ground, we could get off and set up a defensive position. We tried to get off the birds while they were inches above the ground, and very, very quickly because we were extremely vulnerable as were the birds. We didn't like to be sitting ducks, nor did they. I believe the pilots always appreciated our speed. Once all of the birds had safely landed, we would prepare to leave the L.Z. as quickly as we could to disappear into the jungle.

After we had quickly secured the L.Z. and set up a perimeter, we could still see the birds off in the distance, disappearing from sight. It was a heart sinking feeling when our last attachment or physical link to the world would be rapidly disappearing from sight, and we knew that once again, we would be alone and possibly out of support range. And we probably would be the only Americans in the area, with no available help even nearby. All we had was radio communications with the rear.

As I said earlier, it is difficult to place the full terror, excitement, the anticipation, highs and lows into words. We knew the odds were that sooner or later it would be a hot L.Z. We also knew that we might not live to see the next minute or hour. It was somewhat like a roller coaster ride; it's a tremendous rush as you are going through the drops and turns, but the difference is you know you are going to stop safely at the end. The next time you are on a coaster ride, think what it would be like if you didn't know what the end of the ride was like, or if you didn't know if it would crash or not at the end. Then think; what if someone is shooting at me!

An assault, like a firefight, is the biggest high and biggest low in the shortest period of time. We never knew how the beginning would end, how the end would begin, or if there would be an end. All we knew was that when it was over we were mentally drained and glad it was over. It's an experience that I can never forget.

When "show time" was over and we were on the ground, it was then time to disappear off the L.Z. and start the hump to a night defensive position. Typically, the hump after an assault was longer in order to put some distance between the L.Z and us.

One of the problems of being on the first bird in, was the firing of the M-60's on the choppers. As we approached the L.Z. we did not say, "time out, I need to put in ear plugs", nor after we landed could we have stopped to take them out. The piercing noise created by the machine guns firing has created hearing problems for me and many other vets. Ringing in the ears or tinitus, as it is known, never goes away. Even as I am writing this book I am constantly reminded of the assaults, because my ears remind me every minute of every day of the year by their continual ringing.

I was probably average in the number of C.A.'s I had in the Recon platoon and I believe the number I lived through was 57. I cannot begin to remember every single one because of the numbing effect, the highs and lows, mental overload, and the condition of being hardcore. This number also matches what "Pappy", "Wild Bill", "Four Eyes", and "Marty" remember having.

A tired and weary Howard "Pappy" Grabill headed in to the rear.

Hardcore allows you to cope with the situation, remembering or forgetting, because the mind takes over and you cannot control the thought process, and allows you to go on.

Occasionally, the environment was rougher that the assault. I remember one uneventful assault where, as we were preparing to move out, we were attacked by fire ants. Apparently, the rockets from our beloved snakes had hit a colony of ants and they were upset with the world and decided to take it out on us.

Most of our assaults were reasonably uneventful by our standards, except they left us mentally exhausted. Because we traveled in small groups, it was unusual for us to even know if we had a hot L.Z. unless the chopper pilots called us and let us know that they had or were receiving fire on their exit.

There are several theories on why we were so lucky with most of our assaults. I doubt if any single one is correct but combined they make a lot of sense.

The first theory, are the snakes. Undoubtedly, they were a huge deterrent to anyone shooting at us. They could bring the wrath of God on the enemy in seconds. We knew it and so did the N.V.A. I'm sure it would be difficult to shoot at us and take cover at the same time. The appearance of the Cobras was vicious. Slender machines of death with a shark's mouth painted on the nose, poised to bite at a moment's notice.

The second component of the theory equation, was our appearance. The N.V.A. were very intelligent adversaries. They knew the Americans were typically there for a year and then gone, while the N.V.A. were there for the duration or till death, whichever came first. The N.V.A. were like a lot of soldiers, they had binoculars to survey the situation. I think that as they saw the approaching slicks, several things started going through their minds. First was the snakes, but second was probably, why so few helicopters? If it was a Line Company it might be one to two-dozen slicks. A team normally needed two birds, the whole platoon was four, occasionally five at the most. Was this a normal group to attack? Remember, the N.V.A. was there for the duration and small units were usually the better-trained soldiers or an elite unit. So why attack?

We believed they would often times follow us to see where we were headed so later that night they could try to get us with mortars. The N.V.A. weren't in a hurry. They could always wait for easier targets. Also, they could see our uniforms were different than normal. This would reinforce the "elite unit" thought. I refer to this combination as the "Fonzie" theory. If you remember the sitcom "Happy Days", Fonzie was the meanest and toughest guy around and everyone backed down from him, but you never saw him fight. It was his reputation. I think that the N.V.A., looking at a few men in different uniforms were concerned about confrontation because of reputation. Not only that, the N.V.A. had intelligence gathering, the same as the Americans. Very few units operated where we did and our unit was known to be good. I think our reputation, or the reputation of small units, helped to reduce attacks.

Where we operated was also a factor. To be honest, we did not know where we were at all the time. This point needs to be explained some. We had maps but we did not have the whole picture. We knew where we were at on the map but we did not know where that portion of the map was located on the large map of the area of operation. But certain facts were known. One was that, many times we were on the fringe or beyond artillery range. That placed us in portions of the A Shau valley and west of there.

Besides being out of artillery range, sometimes it was difficult to have radio transmissions unless I had the long antenna out and we were on the top of a ridgeline or mountaintop. We were involved in a lot of assaults, and Line Companies were carrying out a lot of assaults, but we never saw any around us or beyond us, ever. Other than my first couple of days in the field, I never saw or heard of any American troops in our area of operation. That reinforces that we were the furthest troops out and probably where we should not have been.

Another point that indicates we were in the N.V.A.'s back yard, was the lack of booby traps. A lot of units hit booby traps, but we didn't. Typically the N.V.A. guarded their front door and did not worry about their backyard, and I believe we were in their backyard much of the time.

Something else that was a dead give away, that we did not think much about at the time, were the helicopters we flew in. Often times, there were no markings on the helicopters to indicate what branch of the military was flying us, or in this case, what branch of the government we were working for. This is another strong hint that we were definitely different or special. So, if you were the enemy, would you attack a small unit coming in that wore different uniforms and flew in unmarked helicopters? Or, wait for easier targets?

I believe that the fact that the war was not at its peak did help improve our chances, but at the same time we were fair game to be taken out, plus a Recon body or Recon P.O.W. carried a high bounty.

Of all the assaults we had there was one that I will never forget, no matter how bad I want to, or how hard I try, or how much I wish I could. Co Pung.

CO PUNG

*T*he following description of the assault on Co Pung is explained reasonably mild. Words cannot describe the emotion or feelings of the events. Too many nights of sleep were lost in writing this book, and to try and place the words on paper to accurately describe the assault would create too much pain. My good friend Gary described it best. It was like having the worst nightmare you could possibly think of and realizing you can't wake up; for 9 straight days. The events of Co Pung created mental stresses beyond belief and mental shut down, which is why it is difficult to remember so much of the assault.

I remember it like yesterday, all of us do. Unfortunately or fortunately, we cannot remember it all, only portions of it. I remember the preparation for the assault well.

One of the few things we got to do that was somewhat fun, was rappelling. Rappelling is sliding down a one hundred-foot rope out of a chopper or a fixed tower. Rappelling was a method of being inserted into an area when there was not an L.Z. established. You make a "Swiss" seat from rope and a "D" ring. Then wrap the rope around the "D" ring and slide away! It was scary the first time we did it but after a few times it became fun to see who could slide down the rope the fastest. And that was the goal, to be fast. Practicing to rappel out of the helicopter was fun because it was a game to us. But the reality of it was that real life rappelling meant the faster you slid down the rope, the better your chances of survival. We practiced at Firebase Jack several times. We practiced there because that was the staging area for the assault on Co Pung Mountain. We had one "live" assault that we rappelled into during the preparation for Co Pung, but the area was reasonably quiet so the risk level wasn't too high.

Beyond a shadow of a doubt, the neatest thing I did in 'Nam, or possibly in my life, was the extraction from the practice rappel insertion. We had been trained using harnesses in Camp Eagle, but the real life extraction was just the opposite of the ride down. The choppers would return with three ropes dangling from underneath. Each rope had two loops on it. The large loop went under your arms and the small one you snapped to your "D" ring, and away you went. It was like being "superman". Flying a few thousand feet in the air and gliding back and forth by moving our arms or legs. It's one of the few things I did in the Army that I would do again. Of course when we had our practice rappel insertion and extraction we had our friends, the Cobras, escorting us.

The freedom of hanging under the helicopter, with the wind in your face and seeing the jungle below, is indescribable. After a while it became hard on one's anatomy but it was still great to do.

Coming back from an extraction by ropes after rappelling in.

Recon practicing rappelling at FB Jack for assault into Co Pung

Unfortunately, we were practicing to rappel into HELL! We had a couple of attempts to go into Co Pung but the weather kept us from going in. It was fortunate that the weather prevented us from rappelling in because we would have been sitting ducks. I remember seeing some awfully big tracer rounds being fired at us and how frightening it was holding a 155 m.m. canister with my rope rolled up on it, knowing that if I had to slide down it might very well be the end of me.

I have heard the number of times we headed towards Co Pung and turned back, because of it being socked in, as being two to five. I know it was at least two. I don't remember the actual figure but all the early attempts were irrelevant compared to the final. I am not even sure why we were taking Co Pung, where Co Pung was, or if the mountain we assaulted was actually Co Pung. I was told the mountain had another name, An Dong Vong, or something similar to that. I assume that I was given the other name being as I was carrying the radio and I was on the first bird in. Co Pung was bombed by every thing we had for about two weeks prior to our landing.

We were told that we would be the first Americans ever to land on Co Pung and the first non-Vietnamese forces since the French were there in 1953 or 1954. I was the second person on the mountain. "Bull" was the first and he was wounded. Co Pung is overlooking the A Shau valley and Laos. It was listed as hill 1615, indicating it was approximately a mile high. We were given a handout stating why we were taking the mountain, but none of it made sense. The number indicates elevation in meters: 1615 is 5298 ½ feet or approximately a mile high.

The "where" of Co Pung may never be completely answered. When I was in the division TOC of the 101st, after I left the field, Co Pung was not shown in the same place as previously described. It was west of the A Shau and south of Khe Sanh. It was in an area of Vietnam that curved up towards Laos and would give the impression it was in Laos. It is sort of like being in Detroit, Michigan. If you go due south out of Detroit, you hit Canada.

The other thing that we remember about leaving Co Pung was the long flight back and I'm pretty sure we crossed the A Shau on the return flight. It is hard to be on the east side of the A Shau, fly east and south, and still cross the A Shau. The "official" report on Co Pung listed it as the second highest peak, and that contradicts the maps. Also, in looking at pictures we have of Co Pung, we can see two other peaks sticking above the clouds. How can it be the second highest and two peaks appear to be higher?

While searching on the Internet, I went to some South Vietnamese web providers that had English on them. I e-mailed them to find out if they knew of, or had heard of Co Pung, and none of them had. I wonder why? Does the name of Co Pung Mountain exist? Some links on the Internet, when the name of Co Pung is typed in, refer to someone with the last name of Pung, but the majority went to sexually oriented links. In Vietnamese, Co translates into "mountain" but I could not find a translation for "Pung".

Today it is irrelevant where it is, because now it is only out of curiosity that I would want to know the location. And regardless of location, the outcome didn't change any.

I even went to the "Stars and Stripes" newspaper on the Internet and e-mailed one of the correspondents. We have copies of clippings showing the Recon platoon but they show no records of an assault on that day or anything referencing the Recon platoon. The correspondent hunted for a couple of weeks and found nothing. Where did we go?

There is also one other detail to consider about the assault. My first day in the Recon platoon we landed on an L.Z. occupied by a Line Company, and that was the only time that had happened. So why was a Recon platoon, whose missions was to quietly search an area and report back, all of a sudden thrust into the role of leading a charge onto a mountain where all hell was supposed to break loose? Doesn't make any sense, does it? There may be an answer and I will place my opinion at the end.

In the final day or two, while we were preparing for the assault at Firebase Jack, there was a small group of men standing around Air America helicopters like they were waiting to go on a mission. Totally unknown to us, and they were not a part of our assault. So, what were they doing there and what was their mission?

Also, during our time at Jack, we were informed we were on standby for a P.O.W. raid but it didn't go down.

To try and put yourself in the right frame of mind for the assault I am getting ready to describe, think about the scenario mentioned earlier of sliding on the ice with a semi jackknifed in front of you. Think about the adrenaline rush, the fear, possibly your last moments alive. And then think about being on a long, icy hill, and you see a jackknifed semi ahead of you, and you know it is too late to stop. What are your thoughts? The soldiers after the 4th bird in had a similar experience, except they knew they were going to be shot at.

April 30th of 1971 is a day those of us in the Recon platoon will never forget, no matter how hard we try or how bad we want to forget. After we had some aborted attempts due to weather, the real thing was about to take place. As usual, I was lined up to be on the first bird in. As we were lining up to go in, I noticed something very much out of the ordinary. First of all, the pilot of the bird I was on was a Major. That in itself indicated something unusual was going on because the pilots were typically 1st Lieutenants, Warrant Officers, or occasionally, a Captain. I don't ever remember a Major leading the pack. And at that time I probably had around 50 assaults.

As we took off, he turned the bird sideways to observe the formation behind us. It was an awesome sight, a sinking, sickly, scary, awesome sight. Too many helicopters for me, and we had eight or ten Cobras escorting us, to soften up the L.Z. All of these added up to a bad omen.

Another bad sign was every seventh or eighth chopper going in was empty except for medics to carry out wounded. This was also a very bad omen. I was wondering what I had gotten myself into. I had been on many assaults but I knew this was to be the worst one yet, and I was hoping it wasn't my last. Later on, I found out the fourth bird in also was piloted by a Major, so I wonder today why we had so much brass flying us that day and how much other brass we had flying us around.

Surprisingly, there was a CBS helicopter in the air above us filming the assault. We heard, several weeks later that it was televised in the States and I would still give both of my testicles to have the footage shot by that helicopter crew! Another question; why was the CBS chopper there and how were they made aware of the event?

Again, as we were approaching Co Pung we saw all kinds of tracer rounds coming at us. We knew this wasn't the typical mom and pop V.C. target practice day. There were too many different colors and different sizes. In looking back, "Four Eyes" and I speculate that the larger tracer rounds were

37m.m. anti-aircraft, something not found on your typical trail. Remember my earlier comments about the highs and lows of an assault? This was much worse because we could feel something was wrong. Even when we took off we could sense the seriousness of this situation. My heart was pounding in my throat. I couldn't swallow if I wanted to! The ride to Co Pung was long so we had plenty of time to contemplate what was going to unfold.

I was thinking to myself as I watched the snakes start to accelerate ahead of us, of all the assaults I had been on we always had a red team (two snakes). What were they expecting that required eight or ten snakes? Besides, for two weeks the area had been pounded by air strikes. The first set of snakes had just cut loose with everything they had and the others were following. The door gunners were getting ready to cut loose with their M-60's. It was almost "show time"!

We positioned our rucks and bodies to exit the bird quickly. My mind was racing faster than it ever had. I double-checked my red smoke grenade to make sure the pin was almost out. I always carried my red smoke grenade on my left ring finger with the pin straightened so I could easily "pop red smoke", indicating we had a hot L.Z. I was thinking to myself, maybe I should just pop red smoke as we hit because I knew it was going to be hot. After a few seconds I decided not to "pop red smoke" even if the L.Z. was hot. For one, the odds of us ever getting off would be greatly reduced if they aborted the assault and odds were, with all the slicks lined up, they would not call it off no matter how hot it was.

We all had the feeling that bad things were going to happen. And they did!

Remember my earlier comments in the combat assault section and the first bird theory? The door gunners were smoking their M-60's as the Major made his approach.

The Major hovered the bird in a bomb crater as close to the ground as he could, to keep from being hit. So we jumped out. "Bull" was the first one off, I was second, and Howard "Pappy" Grabill was behind me. I didn't realize "Pappy" was the one behind me until we reunited in 1999 and we went through the assault step by step. Because of what he described, I knew he was the one behind me. Each time one of the three of us jumped out, the bird went higher and higher. The other two, who were with us on the first bird, were unable to get off because they were too high off the ground. As the three of us were running up the hill I had a terrible feeling. I realized there were only three of us and we were dropped off on the wrong side of the mountain!

As the three of us were running up the mountain, we encountered deserted bunkers with wires running from bunker to bunker. Apparently, the N.V.A. had a permanent bunker complex there, until then. As we got close to the top "Bull" went off to my left and "Pappy" was somewhere between "Bull" and me. I was trying to position myself with the radio, to do whatever I needed to do. I had spent many hours the night before with my S.O.I. and memorized all the frequencies and call signs of the support units, including the arc lights (B-52's), just in case I needed them. As I was crouched down behind rocks, trying to establish communications, I could see rounds (AK-47's or .51 cal.?) hitting above my head in the tree. It was not a wonderful feeling to realize I was alone at the top, on a hot L.Z. and the nearest two people were at least 75 to 100 feet away.

By this time the second bird was on the ground with the Lt. "Wild Bill" was on number three with another radio. The Lt. was supposed to hook up with me for communications, but being as I was on the wrong side of the mountain, he had to wait on "Wild Bill".

Bird three was where problems began. Billy Campbell was carrying the "pig", or M-60 machine gun, for the first time. He figured we might need extra firepower on this mission and he volunteered to carry the "pig". Billy had also turned down a job in the rear to be on this mission because a lot of people assumed this was going to be a "milk run" or an assault that was routine for us. Billy broke a leg jumping out of the bird.

Bird number four had my good friend Gary "Four Eyes" Taylor in it. As they approached the L.Z., his bird was hit and was spinning. He felt something hit him in the chest and it knocked him backward into the bird (that may have possibly saved his life). The bird spun out of control and landed upside down. The prop of the helicopter hit Billy's legs somewhere below the knees, cutting them both off. He was put on the next bird out and taken to a M.A.S.H. (Mobile Army Surgical Hospital). To this day, we don't know much about Billy after that. "Water Buffalo" was also injured in that crash. I was told that the bird had rolled back on him and broke his collarbone. "O.D." had shrapnel from the shattered chopper blades and other injuries.

Gary Taylor's shot down chopper. This is a different view of the same helicopter that is on the back cover.

Gary finally got out of the downed bird and helped the crew get out. He had lost his M-16 in the crash. As he was recovering from the shock of the crash he came across another soldier (part of the crew?) with two M-16's, so he took one of those and went on.

Where I had positioned myself I had a good view of what was going on. I could not see "Bull" or "Pappy" but I could see everything else.

It was probably the most helpless feeling I have ever had, watching that bird crash. It was almost slow motion as it was spinning out of control. No matter what I wanted to do, I was absolutely helpless. All I could do was watch it crash in the crater. I could not see Billy in the crater as the bird went down.

I immediately called the Battalion Commander (Lt. Col. "X") on my radio to inform him of the crash. It was my first transmission and it would at least establish communications. Upon receiving my transmission his question was. Where are you? I replied Co Pung and then I thought to myself. Where is he? He knew I was always on the first bird and he knew my voice well. He was in the command and control ship, directing this assault, and he had no idea where I was? His reply to my location and the crash was and I quote, "roger-out".

The next problem came with bird eight, I believe, or possibly number eleven. I don't remember which number it was. It was overweight, for the altitude, with explosives the engineers needed to use for cleaning off the top of the mountain. I do not know if it was hit or did not have the lift to clear the mountain, but it went over the side of the mountain about twenty-five feet or so from me. Some time later when things quieted down, several of us went down the steep side of the mountain to help the wounded and recover the bodies. It is hard to define a "some time" later, due to the chaos and confusion.

I had sat with most of the men in that chopper a few days earlier, while at Firebase Jack. We were on standby for a rescue mission. We had a chance to visit and tell war stories. I remember the crew chief had a record player wired into the helicopter so he could listen to music while waiting for a mission. He didn't make it. Earlier in the book I referred to nicknames, and one of the reasons for nicknames was a way to distance you mentally from someone, as a way of coping. I didn't know their names, so coping with their crash and deaths wasn't hard.

One of the crew we helped carry up on a stretcher was a mass of congealed blood. He kept sliding out of the stretcher because the mountainside was so steep. When we got him to the top, he passed away. It left several of us quite aggravated at him because he had the nerve to die on us after we risked our lives to bring him back up. How dare he die on us after all that effort!

I think it is appropriate to comment here that I believe it is fortunate that he did pass away. This may sound like a harsh comment and may be difficult for his friends and family to accept, but at best he would have been in a vegetative state during the time he had left.

Wounded being evacuating from Co Pung

One of the crew that made it up on his own had skinned his legs in the crash so badly that both shinbones were exposed.

Because of the chaos, it is nearly impossible to keep all details in order. I believe it was after the recovery work that I found out "Bull" had been shot, as he had gone off to my left during the initial assault. I heard he had been shot going after an N.V.A. machinegun. "Water Buffalo" had broken a collarbone. Billy had lost his legs. "O.D." was injured, and I think we had three or four of the newbys with minor injuries. Another injured soldier was an individual who joined Recon for this mission only. He arrived at Firebase Jack a day or so before the assault on an AIR AMERICA helicopter (CIA owned). He was shot in the groin area and that was the last we saw of him. By the way, why was the CIA delivering "Army" personnel to the Recon platoon for a mission?

Another interesting detail on the assault is in the pictures of the bird that "Four Eyes" was shot down in. There were not any readily identifiable logos or markings on the aircraft. Again, Recon was flying in unidentifiable aircraft. Who did the choppers belong to? Makes you wonder, doesn't it? Gary's bird was piloted by a Major. Why was so much brass flying that day?

After establishing communications with Lt. Col. "X" and helping with the crash site, time seemed to become a blur. It was hard to tell the minutes from the hours. The days seemed to run as one. I do know that it was the last day that I carried the radio. As I understand from "Four Eyes" I dumped it off on him and I think he used it for calling in support. Some of these details are fuzzy because the mind is a mighty powerful organ. Sometimes it limits your memory as you become overloaded from all the strain put on you.

I do not know how many birds made it in after the second one that crashed, if any. The clouds had shifted and we were being socked in. I do know that at the most, there were maybe forty of us there the first two nights. What we didn't know, until almost 28 years later, is the N.V.A. had approximately 950 men (or more) at the base of the mountain. But fortunately, the cloud cover that prevented all the troops from coming in also obscured their view and they did not know how many of us had landed. Twenty to one odds against us don't sound too favorable.

As asked earlier, why is a Recon platoon leading a mission like this?

We removed the M-60's from the downed chopper and set up a defensive position for the duration because we did not know when we would be reinforced, extracted, or if we would even make it out alive. We took trees that were knocked down by bombs or cut down by the engineers to create a defensive position. During the night we could hear movement and assumed we were being probed. We were also mortared that night, and I remember "Pappy" telling me that he attempted to sleep as he was lying between the corpses to keep from being hit by shrapnel. I doubt if any of us there slept for more than ten or fifteen minutes at a time the first two nights.

Our defensive position on Co Pung. Author is in hole with M-60.

A very tired and beleaguered Don "Wild Bill" Corey on Co Pung with the thick, heavy clouds.

The weather at Co Pung always kept us guessing. One minute it was clear, and the next it was cold, cloudy and wet. I believe it was in the mornings when the clouds had settled in the valley during the night that the mountain was a post card picture. The clouds were so thick and rising towards the peak, that you would swear you could walk on them. A clear blue sky and soft, white, fluffy clouds almost made you forget where you were. Almost.

Then the clouds would rise from the warming of the sun, and all of a sudden, we would be standing in a cloud. It was cold and wet. We were socked in until the clouds got higher in the sky, then the reality of where we were set in. The bomb craters were beginning to show their ugliness in pock marking the terrain. I don't ever remember being colder in 'Nam than when we were on Co Pung, and I had been very cold in the monsoons. The wind would cut through us and the clouds would bring in moisture, so we would be standing in a rain cloud. And remember, we had no coats or rain gear or anything to keep us warm!

I believe it was the third day when the weather cleared for reinforcements to arrive, but I don't even remember all the reinforcements arriving. I still don't understand why Recon led the assault, and being as there were only about fifteen of us left, I don't understand why we weren't extracted when the reinforcements arrived. The original mission for Recon was two days on Co Pung. By the way, the official report was that Recon and Bravo Company quickly took Co Pung. Bravo Company arrived on the third day! The official reports also said 5 Americans were killed on the assault. Yet "Pappy" and "Four Eyes" both recall sleeping between approximately 12 body bags. Why the discrepancy?

Tony "Mabby" Mabb and view from Co Pung when weather cleared.

Many things about Co Pung I remember. Many things I don't. I remember the initial assault like it was yesterday. The intensity of the assault and chaos that followed left a person in a state of shock and walking around in a daze. I know in nine days I had to have slept, but I don't remember sleeping. I know I had to have eaten, but I do not remember eating. It was a journey into hell that did not seem to have an ending point. Day one through day nine was a continual blur of events. It was like being on a nine-day telethon. You remember particular events but there is too much for the mind to absorb and process.

We all remember the "thoomps" of incoming mortar rounds and listening for the whistle. It was fortunate that Co Pung was so steep that it made it a difficult target to hit. We had numerous mortar and rocket attacks on us, but I don't know the official count other than there were too many.

As reinforcements arrived, so did better weather and support. Some artillery pieces and personnel were brought in. Plus the mortar platoon was brought to the mountain to return fire, and we had the support from the "fast flyers". You always appreciate watching the fire support on your side working out, and watching it work out on Co Pung was no exception. The mortars and artillery were okay, but we had a great seat for the F-4 jets making their bombing and strafing runs. Because of our altitude, the jets were flying below us and we could see the bombs release and impact. We could feel some of the concussion and feel the heat from the napalm being dropped. The support was close enough on the napalm that, not only did we feel some of the searing heat, but also it would suck the air away from us.

The sounds of the cobra's mini guns were comforting, knowing they were on our side, but listening to the deep roar from 20m.m. cannon on the F-4's was even more impressive.

It is hard to describe the visual effects of a bomb hitting at close range to you. The blast of dirt, trees, dust, debris, the flash of light, everything moving away from the flash, the concussion, are all very hard to paint a picture of. Watching it in a movie has some realistic effects today but is nothing compared to the real thing.

We were lucky that none of us were hit by the shrapnel from the bombing. One of the grunts from the Line Company had been behind a tree, leaning against it. A piece of bomb casing flew over our heads and hit his hand, almost severing a finger. He was waiting for the jets to finish their runs so a bird could come in and medivac him off.

A true sign of being hardcore. The unidentified Recon man in lower left corner is reading or writing a letter, while a 500 pound bomb is exploding less than 150 meters away.

I can still see "Smitty" laying down suppressive fire from his "pig" to help give the jets support. "Smitty" was a Tennessee man who stood about 6'4" and was built or made for carrying the "pig". "Smitty" is the Recon man next to me on the cover picture.

Another thing we appreciated were the manmade earthquakes. The B-52's or "arc lights", as their missions were known. They left an impression not forgotten by friend or foe. At night we would see what appeared to be giant flash bulbs going off in the distance. As we sat there waiting, the ground started to shake continually until all the bombs had exploded. It was truly an awesome sight and feeling as the big jets dropped their bombs; the sky lit up and the earth moved. The N.V.A. referred to them as "silent death" because they would never hear them coming, only the after effects.

View of Co Pung after assault.

View of Co Pung showing extensive damage done by bombing.

Being time was such a blur, it is hard to remember exactly when this event happened, but I think it was after reinforcements had arrived. One of the things to be cautious about when being in an area that has been shelled or bombed, are duds or unexploded ordinance. As mentioned previously, Co Pung was bombed heavily before our assault and one of the types of bombs used were cluster bombs, also known as C.B.U's (U indicates unit). When dropped, the bomb breaks up into scores of smaller bombs or units. These are very effective for anti-personnel use. The individual referred to here was one of the reinforcements that arrived on day three, I believe. I also believe he was an officer. Too many years have passed to remember who it was, plus the incident was very brief in time. Two or three of us were walking back towards the rest of the platoon and this individual was picking up these "things" off the ground and throwing them over the side. We couldn't believe our eyes when we saw what he was doing! We stopped at a safe distance and asked him if he realized what he had in his hand. Obviously he didn't. We explained to him that he was handling small anti-personnel bombs. He carefully placed the one in his hand on the ground and quickly removed himself from the area. He was very fortunate. He could have easily lost an arm, had head or eye injuries, or seriously injured or killed himself.

Co Pung was supposed to have been a two-day mission that turned into a nine-day journey to hell. Biblical hell may have been more pleasant because at least it would have been warmer.

Leaving Co Pung also shows how the blur and chaos affected us. "Pappy" and "Four Eyes" do not remember leaving, while "Wild Bill" and I remember it vividly. It was such a mental relief to leave that it is possible to forget leaving. I know why "Wild Bill" and I remember leaving so well. When the remains of the Recon platoon (remember we had over 25% wounded in the initial assault) were being extracted, we were left behind to wait on another chopper. We were very irritated and upset because we were concerned that we might have to spend another night on the mountain with the grunts and because the entire Recon platoon was gone, except us. I was more than ready to leave because I had been on Co Pung longer than anyone else had at that point. I think we had to wait close to an hour for a bird to pick us up and return us back to Firebase Jack. That is another reason I question the official location of Co Pung. That sure was a long flight back to the firebase and helicopters are not the slowest means of transportation.

To reinforce how much of a blur things were, "Wild Bill" had received a shrapnel wound on his lip and I was unaware of his injury. Until we reunited for the first time I had always thought "Four Eyes" was with me on the last bird out.

Another detail that adds more questions about the location of Co Pung, was the altitude. When "Wild Bill" and I had just left the mountain, the cloud cover below us was heavy so we had good cover. We didn't need to climb higher to evade any small arms fire, or almost any other fire, because the clouds were so thick that we couldn't be seen. I turned around and looked at the altimeter on the control panel and we were flying above 8,000 feet. Why would we be flying 2,700 feet higher than the mountain we just left? Simple math says that if Co Pung was supposedly the second highest peak at approximately 5,298 1/2 feet, then the mountain we left had to be much higher than that.

"Pappy" also told me that he had been talking with the ARVNs that were replacing us. One of the ARVNs told Howie in broken English that, "G.I. come to Laos". "Pappy" responded with "no, G.I. in Vietnam". And their response was "no, G.I. in Laos"!

I also remember sitting in our usual fashion on the slick with my feet hanging out. After a few minutes of flying, the clouds opened up and I could see scores of bomb craters in the valley (A Shau?) below us. I could not believe how high we were, and even though I had been on many assaults and was quite accustomed to sitting with my feet out, it made me a little nervous. Once I took a deep breath and relaxed for a second, then I slid further back into the bird and pulled my feet in.

Several others returned to the rear for a variety of reasons after the assault. They went in for R&R, minor injuries, or dental work. They were greeted with surprise as the R.E.M.F.'s explained to them the Recon platoon had been "red-lined" or had been listed as being wiped out. One of the people that returned to the rear for R&R had a friend in the TOC (Tactical operations center), and in his discussion realized that we were "red-lined" when we took off. Does that make any sense?

I believe this is why we were listed as "red-lined". It was a very convenient way of hiding any history or record of the Recon platoon of "Echo" company; 2/502; 101st Airborne Division. There are records of a Recon platoon but it was listed under HHC or Headquarters Company. Being as we were an elite unit, on a mission under the control of the CIA, we had an "escort" that came in on a CIA owned chopper, and we were flying in on unmarked birds, it made the timing perfect to erase our history. There you have it. We were all listed as killed in action (KIA), but that was only the first time.

It also makes me wonder why we had an "escort" for this mission. It was the first time that a helicopter, openly identified as Air America, had stopped in and dropped off a reinforcement for a mission. We did not have "escorts" join us for any other missions in the past. So what was so interesting about Co Pung that the CIA needed an eyewitness? And if he was there to be an eyewitness, then what did he expect to see? He had to be there for intelligence gathering because he could not have been in a command position. I doubt if his purpose was to evaluate us. Being as Recon did not lead charges such as Co Pung under normal circumstances, an evaluation of us was unlikely. So why was he there? That little piece of the puzzle has bugged me through the years. Obviously he knew more about what was going down than we did.

The handout we received after the mission indicated the raid was to control the high ground around the A Shau valley. If that was the case, why did Air America send in company? There had to be more going on than an ugly assault for them to be interested in Co Pung. So what was it? And remember Recon was flying in unmarked helicopters. It is a shame the Sergeant was wounded on the initial assault. Maybe we could have learned some details of why the people who owned the unmarked choppers had interest in Co Pung.

Also ponder some other facts mentioned earlier. Why was I given a different name for the mountain, and why did the number of Americans killed differ so much from the number "Pappy" and "Four Eyes" had slept between? Why didn't Lt. Co. "X", in his command and control chopper, know where I was if he was watching the assault?

When one steps back and looks at all the details and comments, I believe they add up to some reasonable speculation of why the assault took place. First of all, the weather kept us socked in a lot of the time so the mountain couldn't have been for observation purposes, even though the official report explained that was the reason. In that same thought, being as it was socked in eliminated the use for a communications location because of the weather. You have to remember that in those days we didn't communicate via satellite and the radios weren't that great. The cloud cover made it worthless for communications and observation, so did we take it because it was there? I doubt it.

If you are bombing a mountain for two weeks straight, the enemy is going to assume that you are preparing to assault it. So they will amass troops near it, set up mortars, artillery, anti-aircraft fire, and prepare for a large-scale battle. Remember that there were over 950 enemy troops below us. Just like CBS, they knew we were coming. So, what does all this add up to?

If we were on standby for a P.O.W. raid and it was called off, and just coincidentally there was a small group of unidentifiable troops huddled around some Air America helicopters, the picture possibly becomes clearer.

I think it is possible that Recon's mission was to be a decoy. Earlier in the book, I mentioned we were considered expendable, and I believe that was the plan for us. Bomb the mountain for a couple of weeks, draw in a lot of enemy troops for the big assault, have a big assault, but at the same time slip in a few other "special" troops through the back door and attempt a P.O.W. raid or other special mission. As we take and hold the mountain, we are also consuming a large amount of the N.V.A.'s attention, time and resources. Also, it helps in getting rid of the Recon platoon at the same point in time, as we were listed as being red-lined. Remember that I mentioned earlier that Co Pung was supposed to be a two-day mission that lasted nine days. I don't know how close I am to the right answer but with all of the details adding up, I believe I am on the right track!

The official report mentioned that Recon and Bravo Company quickly took Co Pung Mountain. Recon did take the mountain with a little help from the engineers, but the Line Company arrived on day three.

In retrospect, we were all very fortunate to make it through the first night. The N.V.A. didn't know how many of us made it on the initial assault. If they had only known that approximately 40 of us were defending the mountain, they would have come after us and creamed us. We would have made a valiant stand, but the odds were against us. We were out of artillery range and in a position where we couldn't call in and lie that we had moved. Everyone knew we couldn't move. We were pinned down and surrounded.

After finding some information on the Internet, I learned that Recon, as defined by our organizational set up, was considered a failure by the military. There were too many casualties and too few survivors. Fortunately, I am one of the survivors, as well as my good friends, including "Pappy", "Wild Bill", "Marty", and "Four Eyes". We personally don't think it was a failure. We did what we were supposed to do and did it quite well. If I ever had to do it over again I would do it the same way. A small unit of well-trained people you can trust and depend on. I believe that the term "failure" should revert back to the military and their lack of support and intelligence to handle the operations correctly.

Another item I haven't discussed yet, about the assault on Co Pung, is the fear factor. We were always in fear for our lives, which is why we are all so screwed up today. Once the reality hit of how bad Co Pung was going to be and the assault started, the fear factor increased dramatically. Fear affects everyone differently. I think I was beyond being afraid and more like a zombie. I also believe this is why all of us don't remember as much as we want to about Co Pung. Our brains overloaded and we went into a mental shock that lasted for two or three weeks. None of us can remember details for the two to three week time frame after Co Pung. I was made or became Platoon Sergeant and Platoon Leader after Co Pung, but I don't remember the events happening. I just realized one day that I was running the platoon and wondered how long I had been running it. It's not that important that the time was lost, but it would be nice to remember more of Co Pung and the following two or three weeks.

To describe how the fear factor influenced the others, or me, is beyond words for me. I was scared beyond belief, but because of the chaos, choppers going down, and people being wounded or killed, I can't remember or describe it. The brain is very much like a computer. When a computer becomes overloaded with data or processing capabilities, it shuts down and you have to reboot it. Our brains shut down and told us we had enough. The drawback to the brain is, it can't be rebooted. The information is lost or stored away in places we don't know how to access.

To update this chapter in the book, several details were recently acquired. These facts are placed here because I did not find these details until the last moments before this book was published, and they need to be told and explained.

Co Pung was the American name given to the mountain. An Dong Vong is the Vietnamese for the same mountain. This clears up some of the questions of why I had a second name for the mountain and why the Vietnamese Internet site had no information on it. But it does not explain why "Stars and Stripes" had nothing on the assault.

Co Pung is on the southeast end of the A Shau valley, overlooking Laos as well. Not only did the two names throw me for its location, so did other factors. We knew we took heavy fire going into Co Pung but we were unaware of the enemy's buildup. After our departure, the South Vietnamese captured several .51 caliber machine guns plus many more weapons. The area around Co Pung was also heavily fortified with 23m.m. and 37 m.m. anti-aircraft weapons. Quite possibly, it was one of these .51 caliber machineguns that took out Gary's chopper. Most likely, when I left Co Pung Mountain, the chopper headed north towards Laos to gain altitude and hooked around to the east to make sure it was out of machinegun range. This explains why the altimeter read higher than I expected and also why I believe I crossed the A Shau valley; because I did. And on Co Pung, Laos is to the north. When we were on Co Pung, I don't remember having had any clear days to be able to see the valley below, which also added to the confusion.

So why was it so important to take Co Pung? Most operations had multiple functions. Co Pung was no different. Controlling Co Pung had many advantages. First, when the weather was clear it had an unparalleled view of the A Shau valley. After we left the weather improved, and it was invaluable for fire support. Military intelligence knew the N.V.A. were amassing troops in the area for reasons they were not sure of. One possible reason was for an attack on Hue. The N.V.A. assumed the Americans did not want another blood bath similar to Hamburger hill and FB Ripcord. Based on this assumption, they could have the southern portion of the A Shau for a massive troop build up and march into Hue without much resistance. In fact, after the Americans pulled out of Vietnam, that is exactly what happened. Co Pung was the roadblock for any N.V.A. attempts to attack Hue. Also by controlling Co Pung, the Americans could bring in sensitive communications equipment to monitor the N.V.A.'s radio transmissions and improve their intelligence gathering capabilities.

There is also a silver lining regarding the crash of the fourth chopper.

After we left, a cobra gunship was shot up and it attempted to land on Co Pung. As its tail rudder broke off, the cobra inverted and crashed into the chopper. If Gary's chopper had not been there, the cobra most likely would have gone over the side and both crewmen would have been killed.

I have also found out that before he was evacuated, Billy Campbell fired over 500 rounds from his M-60 machinegun after he lost his legs.

All this information helps us to understand why taking Co Pung was so important, but there is still one primary detail left unexplained. Why was Recon leading the assault?

LIFE AFTER CO PUNG AND BEING KICKED OUT OF THE FIELD

The next two or three weeks after Co Pung are very blurry at best. In looking back, most of us do not or cannot remember events during that time frame. We were probably in a situation that was mundane, but after Co Pung, anything would be considered mundane.

At this point in our lives you have to realize that the brain was still recovering from a severe physical and mental shock, and I don't believe we had mentally caught up with what we had just been through.

I am not sure of what happened to Lt. Barnett. He was with us at Co Pung but now we were down to two small teams, totaling about fourteen or fifteen people. "Pappy" was on R&R, I was the Platoon Leader and "Four Eyes" was the Platoon Sgt. With "Bull", "Water Buffalo", "Wild Bill", and several others in the rear, the Recon platoon was quite thin. To reinforce the state of mind we were in, I do not remember the event or situation causing me to become Platoon Leader or when it exactly happened. I do not know if I was Platoon Leader for a day, a week or how long.

"Pappy" returned from R&R and replaced me as Platoon Leader. He outranked me because Grabill was alphabetically ahead of Price on our promotion orders from N.C.O. School.

The next mission I went on I had "Four Eyes", "Smitty" and his "pig". "Wild Bill" and "Marty" had returned, plus two other newbys, whose names I do not remember. One was a Hispanic guy that was a newby with us and carried a thumper (M-79 grenade launcher), and another kid that carried the radio (I think). I refer to the "young guy" as a kid because I was about three or four months shy of being 22 years old and he was probably 20 at best. I also don't remember if the two newbys were with us on Co Pung or not. The area we were operating in was supposedly "quiet" or had very little enemy activity.

At some point earlier (two weeks to maybe a month at the most), the area had been a hot spot. On a patrol, we came across some rucksacks left behind by a Line Company. Apparently, they had hit heavy contact, dropped all their gear and evacuated the area. We were a little concerned about booby traps but didn't find any. The only problem was in the evacuation. Persistent CS was dropped. Persistent CS is tear gas in a solid form. Persistent CS is basically a time-released form of tear gas. Everytime it would rain, more chemicals were released. The bag I was sitting next to had the appearance of rock salt pellets. Of course, we didn't have gas masks or anything of that sort. For the hardcore Recon platoon, the only thing it did was to make the eyes water and itch, and occasionally you would sneeze as it irritated the nose and throat.

Being the quantities of rucks were greater than the number of Recon men there, we called for help from the mortar platoon. They happened to be on a nearby ridgeline that had a L.Z. on it. I should also state here that this was the first time since I entered the Recon platoon that we had ever set up near the mortar platoon, and I believe it was the only time (other than Co Pung) that I knew of them being in the field.

The mortar platoon consisted primarily of men who couldn't cut it in the field for different reasons. Normally, the Platoon Sgt. and a few others knew their stuff, and the rest just followed orders. Some of the mortar platoon people had egos and absolutely no bush intelligence. I don't remember the number, but I believe three or four of the mortar platoon grunts that helped carry the rucks back to the L.Z. did so without shirts on. They were medivaced out later that evening for CS burns from having the rucks rub against bare skin. I'm not trying to put the mortar platoon down too badly, but as this chapter progresses, they created many problems without realizing it and all of the problems were a result of horseplay.

A couple of days earlier, we had a large number of South Vietnamese Marines hump through our area. I do not know where they were destined to end up, but it was very unusual for us to be anywhere near any other troops, let alone South Vietnamese troops. Being as we were always defensive, we assumed they were being tailed.

My team's mission was to follow a trail back down between the ridgelines and see what we could find, or see if there were any signs of the South Vietnamese being tailed. Always assuming that they were followed and being ready for a firefight. That was our training and experience; always expect problems. The team was also very experienced, with "Four Eyes", "Smitty", "Wild Bill", "Marty", and me, plus the newbys had some experience.

About midday, we had stopped to report our location and give our sit rep (situation report). We were trying to raise the mortar platoon on the radio to give them our location but they did not respond. Fortunately (or unfortunately as you will see later on), we were able to raise battalion and give them our location. Being as it was midday, we broke for a couple of hours till it was time to head out. We tried to raise the mortar platoon again but we were having radio problems, which wasn't totally unusual. The typical tricks of cleaning the contacts with an eraser failed as well as everything else.

In situations like this, the first step was to try and establish if anyone could receive us. To accomplish this, we would transmit and respond with "we are having radio problems, if you can hear us break squelch twice". Breaking squelch twice is done by depressing the handset on the radio for three or four seconds, release, and repeat. This allows us to know that we are transmitting, that they received our transmission and know our location, and that we are okay.

We did not receive any response and we tried to raise battalion again. We still did not receive any response. However, we saw a green pen flare go up from the area of the mortar platoon, so we were assuming they received the transmission. Later on, I found out it was bad timing and horseplay.

Because of the radio problem, we decided to set up where we were for the night and return to the L.Z. the next day. Being as we were always quiet and on the defensive, we didn't think our location was compromised. As the evening wore on, we heard a few M-16 rounds being fired from the L.Z. area. We all assumed the worst and presumed a sapper had attempted to breach the perimeter of the mortar platoon. Remember that these people did not have much jungle or bush savvy. Later on we saw a red pen flare go up from the L.Z. area. Being as red was a danger signal, we had to think something was wrong. We decided to pull a 50% alert to be safe that night. A 50% alert is when every other person is awake on guard, instead of everyone taking their turn.

Now the Recon platoon, as mentioned throughout this book, was always defensive and never traveled light. When I gave up carrying the radio on Co Pung, I added four claymore mines to my ruck and increased my number of hand grenades to eight for defensive reasons. Our goal at night was to put out so much explosives in front of us and around us that if the N.V.A. did stumble upon us, all the explosions and hell breaking loose would give them the impression that they had hit a very large unit, not just seven or eight people.

In the team that night we had approximately fourteen claymores around us, which is more than any Line Company of one hundred would have out. Plus we had "Smitty" and his "pig". There were one thousand rounds between him and his assistant gunner. By the way, "Smitty's" "pig" was always cleaned and ready to "rock and roll". I remember he carried five hundred rounds around his waist, covered with a towel to keep them clean and concealed. You could also place money that every round was linked properly to feed.

The Hispanic newby that carried the thumper carried about eighty rounds for it, so in essence we had our own mortar platoon.

And all of the rest of us carried between 700 and 1000 rounds for their M-16. We were always "loaded for bear". Why not? Our survival depended upon it.

Being as Lt. Col. "X" also heard the shots from the L.Z. area, he assumed we were the ones receiving fire.

They tried to raise us on the radio but because of the problem of it not working, there was no answer; so therefore, he decided we were under fire. If he had called the mortar platoon on the radio he would have found out the firing came from them (if they would have admitted it). But he hadn't.

So somewhere in the midnight range, Lt. Col. "X" decided we needed a radio to make it through the night. Whatever details or facts brought him to make that idiotic conclusion is beyond my comprehension. You have to remember that we were one half of the number 1 rated platoon in the whole 101st Airborne Division! As I have mentioned earlier, I often thought his inexperience or inability made him the enemy as well. In this case he was, and it almost cost him his life.

His belief, as I found out the next day, was that if he flew over the area we were in, we could guide him in with our strobe lights, and he could lower a radio by rope to us. We had small strobe lights for emergency use and they were primarily used to guide choppers in during heavy fog or monsoons, but that only happened only a couple of times to my knowledge. The strobes could be seen for miles on a clear night, and it was a very clear night.

He flew directly over our night defensive position, turned on a spotlight, and unknowingly compromised our position. We quickly took down our ponchos so we couldn't be seen and to eliminate any glare or reflection. At that point our biggest problem became "Smitty", because the chopper was possibly giving our location away, thus putting our lives in jeopardy. "Smitty" wanted to shoot it down. We had to convince him that the pilot was innocent and shooting the bird down would result in artillery being called in on us, or mortars from our own mortar platoon.

It only took glances from "Marty", "Four Eyes", "Wild Bill" and me to decide not to turn on the strobe lights. It was more of a simultaneous look and shaking our heads than anything else. Recon was known to be very defensive and would not give away its location by standing in the middle of the jungle with a strobe light on. The strobes could be seen for a couple of miles, so to turn them on and say "here I am" was neither defensive nor smart. It would be down right stupid!

Lt. Col. "X", in his great wisdom, returned back to the firebase and he reported to the Division T.O.C. that, because he could not find us and drop us a radio, my team had been wiped out and there were no survivors. Pretty good trick, as most of us had already been listed as wiped out about five weeks earlier on Co Pung.

I have always assumed that the pilot of the chopper was ordered by Lt. Col. "X" to fly or be court-martialed. Either that or he was dumber than Lt. Col. "X" was, for he was a bigger target than we were!

All of us stayed awake for the rest of the night. We couldn't have slept if we wanted to.

The next day we started the return up the valley area. We heard some noise and thought it might be the other Recon team. We used signals by rapping on the stock of our M-16s. They responded appropriately and we moved up to them. I think "Hogbody" was walking point. He informed us that Lt. Col. "X" had announced that we had been wiped out without a shot being fired by us. Very hard to believe considering everything we carried. Of course, the other team knew better and refused to believe it.

All of us were extremely upset at Lt. Col. "X" and his antics of the night before. Our adrenaline was so high from being aggravated at Lt. Col. "X", that we probably could have carried two rucks without noticing it.

Upon our return to the L.Z., I insisted upon a confrontation with Lt. Col. "X". Being as he was enraged with me because I did not turn my strobe on for him, he also wanted to have a face-to-face conversation with me.

Lt. Col. "X" was very familiar with Recon and its reputation, and knew me by voice. I had talked to him scores of times on the radio and he knew my voice well enough that we had deleted all formalities on the radio.

A chopper was sent out to take me back to the firebase for my meeting with Lt. Col. "X". I planned to politely explain to him that, because of my field experience and the situation I was in, I was right and he was wrong. And then I would return back to the team. Besides, I had to be right because we all survived!

To begin with, he had assumed the gunfire and red flare were from us. The gunfire was from someone in the mortar platoon who had just cleaned his weapon and wanted to make sure it fired. The red flare was from the guys in the mortar platoon fooling around. But he never radioed them for confirmation of gunfire from our last known location.

In his command bunker, he explained to me that they had no idea where we were. My obvious response was, "how did you know where to fly then?" He explained that the last transmission of mine they had received was a good starting point. Besides, he commented, Recon was famous for moving at night. Obviously I had to straighten his thinking out. I explained that we were famous for making the North Vietnamese and him think we had moved at night, when in fact we were sitting in the same spot all along. That comment did not set well with him.

He asked about the past moves we did at night that allowed him to give clearance for artillery to be called in close to our previous position. I explained that those didn't happen either. We had convinced everyone, including him, that we had moved but we simply stayed put, kept low to duck the shrapnel flying over us, and prayed we didn't get a "short" round. My attitude or arrogance was showing. I knew I was right and he was wrong. I even explained it to him simply; we survived, so that makes me right.

After some other differences of opinions, I asked him if I could have his .45 automatic pistol and turn the lights off. He asked "why"? I asserted that, if he could turn his flashlight on and off a few times and not be shot by me, then I could agree that he was right. Shouldn't be any different than me standing in the jungle with a strobe light on, right? He responded that he wasn't that stupid and I replied, "Well, neither am I".

That pretty much ended the conversation. His final comment was that he didn't need N.C.O.s with my attitude in the field, especially leading Recon. To get the last word in, I commented that if the previous night was an indicator of his leadership abilities then I did not want to be in the field under him! Thus ended my stint in the Recon platoon.

I was on the next chopper back to the rear. I had just been kicked out of the field. A trick that is not easily accomplished!

There is a detail of this incident that I was unaware of until "Wild Bill" and I were talking about the details of this incident 33 ½ years later. Shortly after I was kicked out of the field, he had to go into the rear and he ran into an old friend of his from a Line Company. His friend told him that, the night of the incident, Lt. Col. "X" had the whole Line Company sitting up all night long, with all their gear on an L.Z. They couldn't even go to sleep. Their mission: they were on standby to go in and recover the remains of the wiped out Recon team.

THE LAST TEN WEEKS: THE DIVISION TOC

Well, I managed to get kicked out of the field and sent to the rear. Really, it was kind of scary! As hard as it is to believe, Recon men feel safer in the bush than in the rear. One has to realize that, after a period of time when you are around good people twenty-four hours a day, seven days a week, a strong sense of security and trust develops. That feeling with those people lasts forever.

In the bush I was in my element; the rear was too political and military. We didn't shave, shower, salute, or anything politically correct in the bush. We survived. Not surprisingly, the people in the rear never liked the Recon platoon coming in. The Viet Cong always knew when we were back in camp and the rocket attacks started. The people in the rear felt safer when we were gone because they were not the targets the Viet Cong were after, it was us. When Recon was gone, no rocket attacks. When Recon was in, rocket attacks. That's why the rear echelon did not like seeing us. The Viet Cong and North Vietnamese always wanted to get Recon men. An O'Deuce Recon man carried a bounty that was equivalent to approximately a year's wages, if I remember right.

The rear consisted of the normal rear echelon and all the people that couldn't make it in the bush, the druggies and potheads, the brass, and the R.E.M.F.'s. I figured I would be digging ditches for someone, after managing to get Lt. Col. "X" upset with me, and in the end all I did was offer to shoot him with his own .45 to prove I was right. But I was very hardcore, and getting shorter by the day (short relates to time left in country).

After pulling guard duty for two nights, with a couple of potheads, the company clerk informed me that I was being reassigned to Headquarters Company. That was okay, I guess, it was only a few blocks down the road and I could visit with the Recon guys if they ever came out of the bush. He then explained to me that the Headquarters Company was at Division level. Okay, I thought to myself, dig ditches for higher brass, I can live with that.

Here is another twist and an indicator that the Recon platoon received special treatment. Remember, I had only pulled guard duty and had not talked or interviewed with anyone during those two days. This is also the way it was, not the official version.

The official version was that I had requested a transfer, was interviewed, had the transfer approved and <u>two</u> weeks later I went in for a transfer! This and the following information is from copies of my orders I have kept through the years.

Let us look at some common sense thoughts. First of all, how could I have filled out a transfer form when I was in the bush? Some of this happened during the time when they couldn't raise us on the radio (by the dates on the paperwork), plus I didn't know you could even request a transfer.

Second, the time I interviewed, by the dates on the paperwork, was when I was already doing the job. The paperwork is what I refer to as follow up or catch up versions. I was placed in the position and the documentation followed later; incorrectly, but later. It stated my conduct as excellent, yet I was kicked out of the field by Lt. Colonel "X"! Doesn't add up, does it?

Upon my arrival at the Division headquarters, I was assigned a barracks to sleep in, and checked in. After checking in, I realized things were different than I had expected. The barracks I was assigned to was like being in a hotel after being in the bush. I had a set of bunks to myself with real sheets, a mattress, and get this, a pillow! Actual showers were only half a block away. I could shower every day!

The big surprise came when I was told to report to the Division TOC or Tactical Operations Center. Upon my arrival at the guard shack I was given an I. D. badge with my name and rank on it. I thought something odd was going on and wondered why I was there. I had not interviewed with anyone, yet I was going to work in an air-conditioned bunker, eight feet underground, in a fenced in, restricted area. I had no idea what I would be doing. The people for whom I would be working knew nothing about me except I came from the Recon platoon and was kicked out of the field. How did I get this? Some people would have killed to have a job there! Maybe it was a little status symbol to have a Recon man to empty the trash and sweep the floors.

The next surprise was my assignment. I went down to meet Captain Harrington and Lt. McDaniel (whose names I am not positive of). They were both very pleasant to me, as well as to work for. I was shown a seat on this long bench set up and was informed that I was now the Assistant G-2 Intelligence Sgt. for the 101st Airborne Division. How did I get there? I managed to get Lt. Col. "X" very upset with me, and this was my punishment? I should have made him mad at me a long time before.

As I looked around the area, I noticed signs indicating a Top Secret clearance was required. I didn't know I had one of those. And lo and behold in the Operations (G-3) section was Sgt. Delong, whom also had been in Recon a few months earlier. I knew who he was, but we were not close friends like "Pappy", "Marty", "Wild Bill", "Four Eyes", and I. Interesting, I thought, what are the odds of two Recon guys being in a TOC of maybe fifteen or twenty people? Of all the people they had to choose from, two out of the Recon platoon seemed highly unusual or coincidental.

After the formalities of introductions, Sgt. Delong told me about hearing the report that we had been wiped out a few days earlier. Being a Recon man himself, he had informed everyone that it wasn't possible. He explained that he knew us well, and for us to be wiped out without shots being fired just couldn't happen. I do not remember asking, but I hope he was able to tell the brass, "I told you so!"

Life in the TOC was easy after being in the bush. The shifts were only 12 hours a day, 7 days a week. I heard a lot of complaints from the R.E.M.F.'s, but after being in the bush, this was easy. I typically showered daily after lunch. I also had three hot meals a day, and I didn't miss carrying a ruck. Not only that, I could sleep with both eyes shut! The TOC was air-conditioned, and a refrigerator, with cold pop for sale, was about thirty feet from me. Imagine, cold pop!

My day, compared to the bush, was boring. Daily, the Capt. and the Lt. briefed all the brass, including the Commanding General of the 101st (a two star General). I was the pointer and had a set of starched jungle fatigues just for the briefing. This was where I became suspicious of the location of Co Pung once again. My part of the briefing was to indicate on the map the location of daily events.

After we left Co Pung, other American troops were there for about a month, and then the South Vietnamese took over. The N.V.A. went after the South Vietnamese and they (S.V.) were soundly defeated. This came up during the briefing, so I pointed to Co Pung as it was indicated on the map. But it wasn't in the same place I remembered after the assault.

An interesting thing happened next. When the General asked me how I knew of Co Pung, I simply stated that I was on the first bird in on the assault, and then he smiled. I always wondered what he was thinking and could have told me at that time, but I'll never know.

Two or three weeks after I went into the TOC, I had a visitor from the Recon platoon. "Pappy" was in the rear and had stopped in. What I didn't know, until the reunion, was that he had been asked to take my old position in the Recon platoon. Lt. Col. "X" had explained to "Pappy" how much of a screw-up I was, but "Pappy" defended me, explaining to Lt. Col. "X" that he had known me for a long time and I wasn't a screw-up! I doubt if that set well with Lt. Col. "X", and I am assuming "Pappy" realized it. Unknown to me, he figured that if I got a job in the TOC, so could he. He applied and was offered a position (that would have been 3 from the Recon platoon!) but Lt. Col. "X" hassled him over it. So "Pappy", in typical Recon fashion, was one step ahead of Lt. Col. "X". He handed him his papers for a drop for college (a drop is allowing a soldier to return to college if he has little time left in country). "Pappy" took his college drop and was on his way home a few days later. Way to go "Pappy" and a belated thanks for defending me!

In my last weeks in 'Nam I was awarded the Bronze Star for having been in country for ten months. The officer that was handing out the awards had asked me earlier if I had any other medals coming to me. He would make that part of the ceremony. Being as he was unknown to me, I passed on the idea and went on. I did have other Bronze Stars, Air medals, and other medals coming, but at that time they seemed irrelevant.

At the awards ceremony, which was very informal, I was given my Bronze Star and asked if I had anything to say. A simple "I'm glad it's almost over" sufficed, and on to the next guy. I have no idea what the individual's name was but he was a R.E.M.F. who had worked in the TOC his whole tour. I doubt if he had ever been off Camp Eagle, except for R&R. He was asked if he had any comments after receiving his Bronze Star, and I was sickened by his response.

He proceeded to deliver a spiel on how difficult his tour in Viet Nam had been for him, and he worked in air conditioning most of the time. How obscene! The man's job was probably less dangerous than driving to work every day and he complained about the hardships of being there. Maybe his girl friend had dumped him, but that process had been going on since the building of the pyramids, so that was nothing new. I could also see it in his eyes. There was a lot of sparkle left in them and I knew he hadn't seen anything. Unfortunately, a lot of R.E.M.F.'s gave the impression that 'Nam was difficult and dangerous for them, while in reality the jobs they had State side was more dangerous that their job in 'Nam.

Another interesting item to throw in about the preferential treatment Recon men received, was my second R&R. I had received orders for a standby R&R probably a month after I was in the TOC. That was unusual because of the little amount of time I had left in country. I was asked if I would allow another individual in the Intelligence section to have it, and I could have another. He was a decent enough individual and quite a bit shorter on time than I was. My response was that, as long as I got one, I didn't care. Surprisingly, I received orders shortly thereafter for Sydney, Australia. I couldn't believe it, but I was allowed to go on R&R and I had less than three weeks left before I went home. It was not supposed to happen that way, but I did not argue. I went to Australia and came back to the TOC as a "one digit midget". That means I had less than 10 days left in country. It was nice, but also an indicator of our status. I don't know what the rules were, but I was way too short for an R&R.

The most disappointing thing about being in the TOC was being unable to say good-bye to my close friends in the field. I always thought that left a void in my life. After depending upon each other, for as long as we were in the jungle together, there is a bonding that cannot be described by words. That is why the reunions are so great.

SPECULATION TIME

So why or how did I end up in the 101st Airborne Division Tactical Operations Center? It is all purely speculation, so here is my opinion, and it is only my opinion.

I don't think Lt. Col. "X" had much of a vote in the matter. I don't believe our orders came directly from him to begin with. Also, remember the Battalion Executive Officer (X.O.) always carried a grudge against us. Why? Because I don't think we worked directly for them. They really didn't control us, I don't think. I think we were assigned to the 2/502 so we would look like a normal Army unit, and, in essence, were "subcontracted" out, for lack of a better term, to the 2/502. I believe we flew in helicopters without markings too many times to be a fluke. We all knew who those folks were and for whom they worked. Remember the Sergeant, who was wounded on Co Pung, flew in on Air America and was with us just for that mission. This whole scenario is a typical set up in clandestine operations.

My guess is, we received our orders second-hand through the Battalion Commanding Officer, and he received them from the guys that supplied the unmarked choppers. If we had operated according to procedure, we would have received our orders from our Company Commander. Which we never did, nor did we ever see him. I don't believe I ever talked to our Company Commanding Officer on the radio. While it was true we "lead" the way for the 2/502, normally, where we went, nobody on our side followed. This was especially true after we went back in the field in January of 1971.

I think I was placed in the TOC because I had been in the Recon platoon. Being as Recon was considered the best unit, it only made sense to choose replacements for the TOC from Recon. Some proof of this was that Sergeant Delong, a former Recon man that I knew only slightly, worked in the TOC probably only ten feet from me. And to my knowledge, did not carry the radio in the field.

Being as I carried the radio for a large amount of the time, and also had been the Platoon Sergeant and Platoon Leader briefly, I think I was placed there to see if I had any hints of anything. Or, if I did, to keep me isolated from regular troops so I could not inquire. With the requirement of a top-secret clearance, plus the requirement of having one's name on a list, it necessitated not having conversations with other troops. Another interesting twist; I didn't suspect anything until they placed me there, which aroused my curiosity.

Some things in the TOC did not add up. For example, some missions by certain units could not be placed on the action board or reported during the nightly meeting with the Commanding General. Why? Everyone in the nightly briefing had to have the clearance. In the TOC I could read the report with my clearance of top secret, yet others couldn't? I am quite sure, from what I learned in the TOC, that Recon was one of these units. There are two reasons I believe this. These reports came to me (us) on paper, but the origin was unknown to me. Some of the reports matched action that Recon had been in, or was involved in, based upon information I received from old friends, but I did not receive a single action report on Recon while I was in the TOC. The information matched too closely for coincidence. Plus, where were the action reports for Recon?

I always assumed my top-secret clearance to work in the TOC was an overnight approval. Normally, a background check is done and time did not allow for that unless it was done when I went into Recon originally.

There are too many other loose ends that do not add up. Remember the coincidences between "Pappy" and me? What are the chances of both of us ending up in the Recon platoon the same day, from different units in the South? "Pappy" visited me in the TOC. I didn't know at the time that he had asked for, and received, approval to be transferred to the TOC. That would have made three Recon men in the TOC out of approximately 12 to 15 enlisted men. Considering that a Division normally had over 4,000 men in it, it makes the odds pretty slim to be a fluke. If I had those odds in front of the draft board, I probably wouldn't have been drafted!

Going back to the subject of Co Pung, remember the choppers were not marked. We had more brass flying us in than I had ever seen. Why were we "red-lined" before we hit the ground? And the day before the assault, why did the folks that run Air America deliver a Sergeant to go on the assault with us. That was the first and only time that happened while I was in Recon.

Co Pung was also a mission that Recon should not have been leading. The only analogy I can think of is with a baseball team. It would be the same as sending their ace left handed relief pitcher in at shortstop. It is the wrong person for the job.

We all knew we were good. But did that qualify us for reserve seating in the rear and front row seats at the Bob Hope show? And to jump ahead to today, why is nothing available on us today?

I must state at this point that, regardless of the direct or indirect reporting status of the Recon platoon and whether all the speculation is correct or even close, it was a very elite unit. It was probably the one unit that was considered "the elite of the elite" and it was nice to know that my friends and I were considered that highly. It was a privilege and an honor to be even considered for the Recon platoon, let alone be in it. Considering the very few that were in Recon verses the number of men that served in 'Nam, you can see why it was considered the elite of the elite.

If I had to do it over, I would want to do it the same way with the same group of people, except I would like to know the facts up front.

COMING HOME AND BEING NORMAL

I was like thousands of other G.I.'s returning home from 'Nam. I didn't admit it. Our families were always glad to see us come home and so were a few old friends, but that was about it. Being in 'Nam was an unpopular situation because of the protesting and politics involved. Most people looked down on us and many people referred to 'Nam vets as baby killers. So once we hit the world we acted like we just crawled out of the woodwork, had been on vacation, or just moved to town. All of a sudden we were just there.

After a few days of acclimating myself to normal sleep, eating civilian food, and not being in a combat zone, I started to try and fit into society again. It was very tough to do. First, there was the time warp to contend with. Everyone around me commented on how I had changed, but everyone around me forgot that the world had changed as well during our absence. They were part of the world as it changed, so they didn't see any difference, where those of us returning did.

People do not realize how difficult it is to be in a combat zone one day and a few days later, be in civilization. I was fortunate because I had a few weeks to "come down" from being in the bush, but it was still tough. Very few people, other than vets, can fathom the mind-boggling task of being in the bush, and a week later, returning to the world. We were used to carrying a weapon, ready to open up to "rock-n-roll" at the bat of an eyelash, sleeping in the mud, or frying in the sun and smelling worse than old tennis shoes. All of which society frowns upon. It was such a culture shock to step out of Vietnam and into the States in such a short period of time. Even trivial things, or things we take for granted, took time and adjustment to try and get back to normal.

A good example of this was going to the bathroom. In 'Nam and in the bush, you would simply find a tree or a spot and relieve yourself. In the rear areas it was more civilized, but still quite crude compared to the world. The urinals, for lack of a term, were a metal culvert half standing on end and placed on a hole filled with stone. It was limed daily to sanitize it. If you needed to relieve yourself, it was a matter of standing between the barracks or buildings, and urinating in the culvert. You lost a lot of your modesty because anyone and everyone would be walking by when you were relieving yourself. The other function was similar to the turn of the century; we had outhouses.

One cannot imagine the number of times when, having to relieve myself, I started to unzip my pants on the spot while in public. It took awhile to remember that, we now had devices that flushed, and I couldn't go just anywhere. I am sure that people stared at me a lot of the time because of the way I would walk down the street or be in a store. The defensive side of me was still strong and I was always looking about and keeping my spacing between people.

Some things were great to adjust to, like going to a fast food restaurant and driving up to the speaker to order fries, a hamburger, and a Coke. Driving was also enjoyable but it was a very strange feeling to drive again. The drawback of automobiles was that cars are cars, and one occasionally would backfire in the seventies. So many times I would be somewhere and a car would backfire. I would either have to pick myself up from the ground if there wasn't any cover, or if there was cover I would freeze in place. I always got the strangest looks when that happened, but I was only one of many thousand G.I.'s that received looks like that.

One of the greatest things I was able to readjust to was taking a hot shower. After going for months without a shower in 'Nam, it was fantastic to be able to bathe daily. Sometimes, no matter how hard I scrubbed, I felt I couldn't get the jungle off of me. A full two years after I returned home, I had people at my work complain I had body odor. I used to tell them that it was the cologne I had picked up when in Thailand on R&R. In reality it, was probably the jungle still oozing out of me. I bathed daily, but with so much time in the bush without showering, I probably had fungus, crud, or whatever in my body still working its way out or still growing on me.

I was trying to acclimate myself to the world and become "normal". First of all, what is normal? That is a question I still struggle with today. But in the seventies, being normal and single at the age of 22 meant having a job, a car, a home, a girl friend, getting married, and having a family. Maybe not in that particular order, but that was the general description of a "normal" young adult. But in the definition of being normal, someone left out part of the ingredients to the formula for 'Nam vets. I don't believe the term "normal" included key ingredients such as: still being hardcore and defensive, sleeping with one eye open, flashbacks, being emotionless, being listed as killed in action twice, drinking out of human skulls, or a few other things. Look into the vet's eyes and notice the faraway look and try to imagine what he went through to get there. How can a person resume to being normal after that? No one can. You couldn't, and I can't!

There we were, 'Nam vets, returning by the thousands and being treated as though we had never left, with society looking at us and thinking; "you shall now return to normal". What a crock! So many vets were "swept under the rug" and kept out of sight because of the way they acted or because of their problems. Society couldn't accept our ways, our attitude, and the way we changed, but we were to accept society the way it was. I couldn't even think normal or look at people in a normal way. But I was supposed to act normal? The job portion of returning home was easy for me. I returned to my previous job and tried to pick up the pieces. I knew I didn't fit in anymore and I was different now, but I was too proud, too deep in denial, and hardcore to admit it. I was just trying to readjust. I got up, went to work, and when people asked what I did in 'Nam, I simply answered, "I was there". The car portion came easy, and after that, things became a struggle.

I started dating, but it was much different than before I went to 'Nam. It wasn't an age thing or the fact that a lot of the people were now married. To me, it was trying to fit into society instead of being part of it (somewhat like the square peg in a round hole comparison). I think the dating scene was an attempt to become normal, as well as a hormone thing. After being in the jungle for such an extended period, the opposite sex obviously had an appeal. Besides, after sleeping back to back with "Four Eyes" for weeks on end to keep warm, the opposite sex had a lot of appeal. But the downfall of this situation become very obvious: it was called a lack of emotion. Many people, including me, for a long period of time have confused lust for love. Lust makes you feel good for a while and it fills a void. Love is supposed to last forever. This is probably one of the reasons so many 'Nam vets are divorced. I was trying to fill some voids in my life and be normal. But there were many voids to fill and many of them I didn't even realize or recognize. As I reflect back, most of us looked at getting married as just another mission to complete. It wasn't love or anything close to it. It was just another mission.

I dated around for a while and ended up getting married, because that was the normal thing to do. I wasn't in love but in lust. To be in love, you need to have the emotional strings attached, and they had been severed long ago. If you get along with someone that means everything is okay. Right? After the jungle, being with a female was an enjoyable situation, and after the struggles of war, an enjoyable situation was a pleasant change. I had already bought a house, so marriage was the next logical step in being normal. Right?

When I was young and still in a mental state of shock from being in 'Nam, I was naïve to what I really went through and what it had done to me. I thought I was adjusting normally, but I wasn't smart enough to figure it out.

I don't feel bad about not figuring it out because a lot of 'Nam vets didn't, nor did about 98% of society, and probably 99.5 % of the analysts, therapists and shrinks didn't understand it either.

I thought I was okay, and the hints of struggle I had were being pawned off as adjusting to society because of the time warp syndrome. Again, I was very wrong on that.

After I was married for a period of time, it was time to have a family, the next logical step in becoming normal. Correct? I already had a job, car, a house, and I was married, so it was family time.

During birth there were problems. My daughter, Janae, was born with her umbilical cord around her neck and suffered brain damage, and eventually a seizure disorder. My wife at the time always disputed the doctors' analysis because Janae had seizures before birth. This fact always made me wonder if it was from the effects of Agent Orange, being we were in it on numerous occasions. God only knows the answer to that question. Janae died 31 months later. I believe that also finished off the marriage. It would have never lasted because of my hardcore state of mind. It was the major event that accelerated the divorce. We had another daughter, Erin. She was healthy and normal, but unfortunately I wasn't "normal" by the standards of society at the time, and never will be.

If you change the name of spouses and towns and remove the death of a child, this story of returning home is the same one told by thousands and thousands of vets. Remove getting married and it fits many more thousands that were already married, but their spouse had "change" to contend with as well.

For thirty years or more, many 'Nam vets have tried to fit into society and become normal citizens, but, unfortunately, society doesn't recognize many of our survival criteria as "normal" for society. I am only normal today when I am around other combat vets!

Could you consider yourself normal after waking up in the middle of the night, thirty years after you left 'Nam, trying to figure out if you are still in 'Nam, as you try to find your weapon? Could you be normal if you had over 50 C.A.'s under your belt and was left in the jungle for what seemed to be an eternity? Or how about all the ingredients that made us hardcore and immune to emotion; could you be normal after that? How many normal people would drink out of a skull like it was a coffee cup and think nothing of it?

Will the 'Nam combat vet, who has seen more and done more than God ever intended, ever be considered "normal"? Look into his eyes because the eyes tell it all: the answer is told in the blank stare. Not today, not tomorrow, not next week, nor next year; the answer is simple.... not in his lifetime! And if you need proof of the answer, look at all the combat vets that carry "baggage" or problems.

SAVING PRIVATE RYAN

When the movie "Saving Private Ryan" was released on video we (me and my soon to be second ex-wife) rented the movie and watched it at home. I was nervous about the opening because I had heard it was pretty intense. It was! I have to admit that Spielberg did a great job of opening people's eyes to the horrors of war. The scenes of limbs being lost or a soldier carrying a portion of another soldier was particularly appropriate.

My soon to be ex-wife always thought that P.T.S.D. (post traumatic stress disorder) was a name given to an imaginary disorder to allow 'Nam vets to have a reason to hide behind their actions or to act the way they do. She once told a marriage counselor and me that her college days were more difficult than my days in Vietnam were! And actually she had the answer absolutely, perfectly right! *Because she, as well as millions of Americans, don't have the foggiest idea of what the vet that was in the jungle had been through.*

Throughout the intense beginning I mentioned several times about the memories that those veterans of WW2 must carry, and the nightmares of it. No wonder they can never forget, I commented on many occasions. She agreed with the train of thought of the horrors and nightmares that these men carried, and still carry today. At the end of the movie, she was unaware that all my comments were a set up to defend Vietnam vets.

Most people that watched the movie were sickened or reminded how horrible and destructive a war is, and rightfully so. A war is horrible and destructive; regardless of what year it happened, where it was, or if you were the winner or loser! Just ask any grieving widow, parent, or relation on the winning side if war isn't terrible. My set up and response to her was (and to everyone reading this book is), we didn't storm beaches in 'Nam, we didn't have them, but we assaulted mountains. We assaulted on a smaller scale, while WW2 was on a larger scale. Regardless, the results were the same; young men died and young men suffered! Parents, spouses, children, brothers, sisters and grandparents suffered. Regardless of which war it was!

Remember the scene of a soldier carrying a limb? Remember earlier in the book that Billy lost his legs? Different time, different place, different wars but the results are the same.

Recall the scene of a soldier carrying half of a body? I have a Marine friend who told me the story of his friend being blown in half by an RPG (rocket propelled grenade) round. The lower half was next to him and he had to retrieve the upper half the next day so both portions could be buried together. As he was telling me the story, he looked at his wrist to see the bracelet bearing his friend's name on it. I could see it in his eyes. There was no smile, only sorrow in his voice as he talked about the "hero" that was killed. I know he has seen more and done more than he wanted to. The eyes tell it all! Regardless of what war it was, the results were the same.

The point is, that even though Vietnam was an unpopular war, it was still a war; young men died and young men suffered. Families and friends suffered and grieved as well. And today we still suffer from various side effects, chemical effects, flashbacks, and many other things. Even if you didn't agree with the war, you have to realize the effects are real and accept the results.

P.T.S.D. AND THE BROTHERHOOD

P.T.S.D. stands for post-traumatic stress disorder; pretty much self-explanatory to this point. My first comment is, P.T.S.D. is not specific to a war, to being shot at or from being in combat. It refers to the effects from trauma and stress. If it were solely for 'Nam vets, it would be P.T.S.D. Vietnam; but it is not. Also, to fully detail P.T.S.D. would take a complete book of its own, so these are my very abbreviated comments and opinions.

I start this subject needing to clarify the acronym. Someone who was beaten, mugged, brutally raped, or encountered other trauma, probably suffers from P.T.S.D. But at this point, many of the similarities end. Possibly the closest civilian P.T.S.D. to 'Nam vets are police that have been in shootouts. Fortunately for them, they didn't live in the jungle, carry a ruck, have combat assaults, or hump the bush, so their versions are quite mild.

I should also state I am not an expert on P.T.S.D., but since I have lived with it in various stages for 30 years, I am versed in it and pretty much understand it.

Everything so far in this book actually defines what we went through to acquire P.T.S.D., the results thereof, and many symptoms or signs of P.T.S.D. Notice how the 'Nam vet acts or doesn't react, and look into his eyes, that will pretty much tell you if he most likely has P.T.S.D. Being hardcore goes hand in hand with P.T.S.D. If you are truly hardcore, then you are going to have P.T.S.D. It is like having the flu; the fever goes with it and you do not separate the two.

P.T.S.D has a lot of common traits similar to allergies. Not all allergies are created equal, some are stronger than others, some are weaker. They affect people differently. They are not all caused by the same pollen. Like P.T.S.D., some allergies are hard to diagnose. The point being made here is that P.T.S.D. affects some combat vets more than others. It affects them differently because of personality, their age in 'Nam, their upbringing, the experiences they had in 'Nam, how mentally adjusted they are, how smart they are in recognizing it or how deeply in denial they are. There are many different factors to the equation in determining the effect of P.T.S.D. on the vet. It goes back to the person mugged, traumatized, or raped; different circumstances in different situations.

I know of some 'Nam vets who suffer severely from P.T.S.D. They would have suffered almost as badly if they had never made it to 'Nam. Their genetic code, personal make up, or whatever determines mental strength and understanding of stress, were different enough that they would have suffered from P.T.S.D. after being in a fight at the local bar three blocks from the trailer park they lived in.

Some vets become violent, some withdraw, some need medication, some can never work again, some can't handle being around people, and some revert back to what got them there, going back to being hardcore and defensive. There are many reactions to the situations and it is difficult or impossible to understand all of them.

First of all, you have to understand, it is real! It is not made up or fantasized! I did not understand it when I returned from 'Nam nor did I even believe in it. I was too bull-headed or naïve to realize it.

P.T.S.D. is something that stays with you forever, as far as I am concerned. If you don't believe me, ask the vets of WW2 and those involved with "Private Ryan". They still carry the combat stress long after their war was over, as well as the nightmares that went with it, and that was long before 'Nam.

P.T.S.D. was also a problem of WW2 and Korea, but it wasn't labeled as such. I have watched several shows with WW2 vets reliving Normandy and other beaches or landings. The tears were real as well as their nightmares. As they told their story, you could see it in their eyes!

I don't believe you cure P.T.S.D.; you have to recognize the problem and treat it based upon all the symptoms and signals, just like allergies. Then you learn how to cope with it. I know that you don't "take 2 aspirins and call me in the morning" for allergies, nor do vets with P.T.S.D. need to be treated the same. It is no different than a person who was beaten or mugged. Would a doctor tell them to take two aspirin and call him in the morning? How about a person that has unexpectedly lost a loved one? All the cases relate to individuals with varying degrees of P.T.S.D., but society, or the overall population, has sympathy in understanding brutality, muggings and mourning because these are centuries old conditions. Plus they are approved by society because they are common. People that have been through these conditions are not told to take two aspirins and go on, nor are these people "swept under the rug". Everyone knows that to recover from being mugged, raped, or beaten, and going through mourning, takes time. Society needs to realize that the vet with P.T.S.D. needs the time and space to cope with the condition.

I handled my form of P.T.S.D. much like an alcoholic would handle his drinking problem. I was in denial for 30 years and simply told people that I needed to be alone or was having a bad day. Really, I was trying to have enough mental room to cope with the day and my past. I knew I had a problem, but facing it and bringing it into the open was a different story.

Many 'Nam vets have P.T.S.D. and are unaware of it or, most likely, in denial and don't want to talk about it. As a personal opinion, it is not your (our) place to question or query whether they suffer from it. That is between the vet and a professional, or another vet that they can confide in.

When you talk to a vet and he tells you that he has P.T.S.D. or you suspect he has and he doesn't mention it, look into his eyes when he talks about 'Nam. The eyes tell it all!

That is one of the many reasons 'Nam vets talk to one another. The 'Nam "brother" understands more so than the average person and the vet feels comfortable in talking to another vet.

In commenting that vets should and do confide in other vets, brings up the subject of "brotherhood". There is an interesting bond among combat vets. A 'Nam vet can be married for fifteen or twenty years or know a neighbor for the same length of time and he will not tell them much about 'Nam. But should a total stranger introduce himself to the vet and they realize the other is a combat vet, they become immediate "old friends". Telling each other stories that their wives, or friends of old, have not heard. It is irrelevant whether they were a "grunt" (Army) or a "jarhead" (Marine).

I had many experiences with this situation. Some of my best friends in the Midwest were individuals whom, after a brief conversation, I realized were 'Nam vets. Many of the normal social barriers were dropped and great conversations proceeded. I believe this was because they knew that we both spoke the same language and shared common experiences that only we could understand. Much like two women discussing childbirth; common experiences and common language.

When I was in Indiana, I met with an insurance salesman regarding my retirement accounts; which is something I abhor. Five minutes into the conversation we realized we were both 'Nam combat vets, and the subject changed to our past. From that point on, we became the best of friends and met on a regular basis for dinner. It was an opportunity for us to tell our stories and get it out of our system, plus relieve some of the internal mental pressure.

I moved to the West just prior to writing this book, and the experiences here are similar. I was standing on my property next to the road, and an individual drove by wearing a 'Nam hat. I flagged him down and asked him "who were you with"? He replied that he was with the Marines, and then I returned with my reply of Recon 2/502. After a smile, a handshake, and a mutual "welcome home", we are automatic friends. The next evening he stopped down and we talked for hours. This also happened with one of the cement crew who was pouring my floor. Upon finding out that he was a 'Nam vet, and a few minutes of conversation, we are like old friends.

So, why does this happen? I believe that when two combat vets meet there is an interaction of past experiences. They can tell by the eyes! Two vets can look at each other and tell by the look in their eyes and the tone of their voice if they have been to Hell and back!

The reason I place this with the P.T.S.D. comments is because I believe this is part of the coping mechanism or a resource for us to vent to. The 'Nam vet needs other vets to talk to because they are on a similar level or understanding. They can relate to each other because of common experiences.

I would say that it is part of the healing process but the terminology is wrong. Certain wounds you recover from completely, like a broken arm or leg, a cut, or minor surgeries. I do not believe you heal from the deep wounds of war. Some of the superficial ones you do, but when you look in the eyes of a WW2, Korean or Vietnam vet and they carry that faraway stare, or at times appear as if no one is home, then they are coping, not healing!

This is not to say that their spouses cannot understand them, but it relates back to women and childbirth. A woman can explain childbirth to a man and he can understand it, but because he has not experienced it, he cannot comprehend it the same as another mother could. It is the same with the vet; the wife can understand it, but she cannot comprehend it.

I often thought there should be a course for wives to study, and learn how to work or deal with their husband and the problems associated with the combat vet. It makes sense, but that is probably why there isn't one, because it does make sense.

THE REUNIONS: 1999 & 2000

After much searching on the Internet and a stroke of luck, I ran across an ad placed by the wife of Gary "Four Eyes" Taylor in the "US Army lost and found" web site. After a letter and a phone call, I was in touch with an old friend. It was one of the most memorable moments for me. Finally, I could talk to someone that believed me because he was there also. We talked for well over an hour, maybe two, but what a relief! Someone finally believed me! But I was also saddened by his comments on his health. We talked for hours in the following weeks because now we could share our problems of the past. We both trusted each other and believed each other because we were there together.

I was able to take a couple of days off from work and go visit with him. It was amazing how alike we acted and reacted. After 27 ½ years, we had a lot of reminiscing to do and war stories to retell. His wife could never comprehend he was shot down in a helicopter, because Gary never had visual proof of the incident. I had sent Gary copies of the pictures I had from 'Nam and one of them was the crashed chopper. When I arrived at his house, there was an 8 X 10 of it hanging on their living room wall, and she now understood.

The weekend of Thanksgiving in 1998, I found Don "Wild Bill" Corey and Howard "Pappy" Grabill. "Wild Bill" didn't recognize my real name. Only when I mentioned my nickname did he know who I was. Amazingly, when I called Howard I got his answering machine and I recognized his voice. After many phone calls, we planned for a reunion in Indianapolis in March of 1999, and what a reunion it was!

When I found Don, I was amazed to find that he lived only an hour and a half from me! We got together for dinner shortly thereafter and spent several hours in a restaurant reminiscing. Not only that, I had been within ten miles of his house on at least a dozen occasions visiting some friends and didn't even know it!

The reunion in Indianapolis was fantastic. It was like old times. Don and I picked Gary up at the airport and we went to have a late lunch while waiting for Howard. About 45 minutes after we sat down to eat, we saw a figure approaching from about 200 feet away and we all recognized Howard.

Howard "Pappy" Grabill, Don "Wild Bill" Corey, Richard "Lambchops" Price and Gary "Four Eyes" Taylor in Indianapolis.

The only way to describe the meeting was magical. As we sat in the restaurant it was as if the air was electrified. There was a feeling or aura in the room that was so thick you could cut it with a knife! As we sat reminiscing with war stories and catching up on the last 28 years, we all realized that part of the magical feeling was that we felt safe again. The security and trust from 28 years ago had never dwindled. We all knew that someone else was watching their back, and the security we felt in 'Nam was back. It was undoubtedly the best weekend any of us had had in 28 years. We sat in a large hotel room and retold war stories and relived events to try and remember details. The bond we carried in 'Nam was still there. After so many years of holding back the past, we were finally able to start unloading the baggage and talk about it. We could finally talk about what we had gone through with others that were there. There weren't any of the usual comments that might have been interjected by other vets. Instead, there was much head nodding, confirming the comment, and other details added. Such a great time!

Later in 1999, I found Hector "Marty" Martinez. Hector lived only a couple of hours from me in the Chicago area, so we managed to have dinner one Saturday in Indiana. I recognized him as he pulled in the parking lot of the restaurant. As we started talking, it was obvious that he had a lot of the past bottled up that needed to come out. All his wife could do was to take it all in and enjoy two old friends reminiscing. We could converse with each other for the same reasons Gary and I could talk about it. It was because we had been through hell together and back, and we believed each other.

In April of 2000, "Marty", "Wild Bill", and "Four Eyes" met at my house. Again, the magic was there as well as the stories and smiles. Howard was unable to attend due to his mother being sick.

The reason for bringing up the reunions in this book is to explain why 'Nam vets talk and retell the same stories. It is part of the coping process. Invariably when Howard, Don, Gary or I talk, the subject of Co Pung comes up.

It is not because we are reliving it, as it may sound, or as people may think, but it is how we cope with it. We remind each other how fortunate we are to be alive today (to my knowledge Don, Gary and I were listed as killed in action twice at Division level and Howard and Hector once), and that the things we did were right, and we did the right things to stay alive. People need to know that when we talk about places like Co Pung, or drinking out of skulls, or the environment, we are helping ourselves. It's when we don't talk and things get bottled up that problems occur. Much of what we discussed had been bottled up for 28 years because we didn't talk to other vets about it, because no one believed us.

Another benefit is peace of mind, or releasing old baggage. Hector carried around the guilt that he was responsible for Billy losing his legs because he (Hector) was supposed to be in Billy's place and Billy was supposed to be in the rear taking a leadership course. Hector thought he had bumped ahead of Billy. Until we met at my house, he felt responsible. After Don told him that Billy had volunteered to be there and wanted to be there, Hector had a huge burden lifted off his mind that he had carried for 29 years! That is why it is good for 'Nam vets to talk about it and get it out!

Another interesting piece of the conversation, or in this case, lack of conversation is "between" times. That is, the time after 'Nam till now. We had very little discussion of what our lives were after 'Nam. We discussed the usuals of being married, having kids, being divorced; the basic stuff. But not much detail was given. Howard drove for UPS, Don was a lineman part of the time, Gary stayed in the Army, Hector was a manager, and I was a manager. Other than that, I couldn't tell you much about their lives. It was because we did not share that time frame with each other.

The time we had together in 'Nam is what we talked about because that is what we shared. Because that short portion of our lives was filled with so much concentrated stress, hardships, insanity, and mental anguish, that portion of our lives changed and affected us forever. Because of the type of group we were in, we could only share these thoughts and conversations with each other and feel comfortable with the discussion. And after 28 years or more, it was great to have many conversations with old friends that I had been to hell and back with, knowing that when the conversations were over, we all felt better and relieved.

I also have found "Doc" McGuire, Alton Mabb, and Dan O'Doughtery. I have had conversations with the three of them and hopefully, all the surviving Recon men can reunite someday.

Hector "Marty" Martinez and Tony "Mabby" Mabb at a Florida reunion of 2004.

Dan "OD" O'Doughtery at Florida reunion of 2004.

FLASHBACKS, BAD DREAMS, AGENT ORANGE AND OTHER LINGERING EFFECTS

Nightmares, bad dreams, and flashbacks are basically the same problem, but in different forms. Most combat vets have nightmares or bad dreams; they are all different but have common denominators, past events or past fears. But so does everyone else at some point in their lives. The big difference is the intensity, frequency and trauma of the dream. We normally regress back into the subconscious and pull up a stressful situation or fear and relive it on a regular basis, sometimes with variations. The flashbacks are bad dreams, except that one is wide-awake.

Most times a "trigger" or event will trip a flashback or bad dream. A particular noise or odor can also trick the mind and we regress back. One common noise that triggers a flashback is a car backfiring or a noise that reminds the brain of gunfire. Another common trigger is The 4th of July fireworks. Many people will buy the aerial or mortar type of fireworks that are fired from tubes. These have the same sound as a mortar round being fired like we heard in 'Nam. If I go to a fireworks demonstration that is restricted to fireworks being professionally fired in a restricted area, such as a football field and in front of me, then I am somewhat okay. If I go to a fairground or similar open area, I must convince myself everything is okay before I go. But, if I get caught off guard by someone behind me firing a mortar type of fireworks, I sleep with one eye open for a couple of weeks. It is unplanned to sleep lightly but it is part of the defense mechanism.

I have mentioned how certain noises can trigger flashbacks. Many young kids or young adults try to draw attention to themselves with loud stereos in their cars. To make it worse, the current trend of music is with very heavy bass. With my damaged hearing, I normally feel the music with heavy bass before I hear it. What these young individuals do not realize is the damage they are doing to their hearing as well as the occupants in the vehicle. The "jarhead" 'Nam vet that lives down the road has a daughter that likes the loud music, and I know he has asked her to turn it down because it would have caused problems for him as well. I am assuming she did not listen to him because she could not understand why it was a problem. One hot summer day, I was in my side yard working, doing clean up of some brush. At that point on my property, I am somewhat in line with the road before it curves. All of a sudden, I could feel a rumbling coming towards me. It felt like distant explosions coming closer. I felt the boom, boom, boom of what appeared to be an Arc Light (B-52 strike) coming towards me. The anxiety from what was happening started to take over and I got very nervous, scared, and confused. My brain throws me in mass confusion because, one second everything is fine, then all of a sudden I believe I am in the path of an Arc Light, and now I don't know where I am or what year it is! As the boom, boom, boom got closer I started to freak out because I didn't think I could get out of the way, plus I was so confused and in a time warp about what was happening. A few seconds later I started hearing music, and then my brain started to realize what was happening and that the boom, boom, boom was really music. Once I totally came back to the here and now, I was okay. The next day when I was taking a walk, I stopped her on the road and politely explained what it did to me and how much it rattled me. I asked her that if from now on, she would turn her stereo off when she reached a point in the road that is about a mile from my house, and not turn it back on till she passed that point on her return to home. I thanked her as she left, and I also thank her because it has been over a year and I have not heard the boom, boom, boom.

Another common trigger is movies. Watching a movie is supposed to be entertaining, but some movie plots have scenes that trigger flashbacks or sleeping with one eye open. If a combat vet is watching a movie and is unaware that there is a scene relating to Vietnam and firefights, the flashback starts or he sleeps with one eye open for several days and the nightmares begin. I know of some 'Nam vets that rarely watch movies because of this. Fortunately, the frequency of these can diminish (but not always) with time but they never totally leave. There is not much we can do about them, except hope that time helps. But they can also return in a heartbeat if a trigger or event trips the vet. When the flashback or nightmares happen, they can be the most frightening and terrible or paralyzing event.

This is one of the main reasons for me becoming a recluse; to remove as many "triggers" from my life as possible. That is the reason I don't watch broadcast or live TV, read papers, or listen to the radio. Less "triggers" equate to fewer bad dreams or nightmares. But even removing myself from most "triggers" does not eliminate nightmares or bad dreams. They will always be there to rattle my subconscious mind and play tricks on my conscious mind.

Because I was a L.R.R.P. or Recon man and always on defense, I tried to stay still or calm until I determined what to do. There are times I wake up in bed, soaked in sweat, and I don't know if I am in 'Nam, where I am, or what year it is. I lay motionless, trying to find my weapon, trying to figure out where I am, if I am in danger or if someone is out there. I might only lie in bed for minutes, but it seems like hours as I am in a twilight sleep, trying to collect my thoughts and analyze the situation. Then I eventually see the large red L.E.D.'s of the clock, and then I'm okay. I always told my ex-wife that I wanted that clock because the numbers were easier to see. That was only partially true, after one of the dreams the larger readout was easier to find.

Most people cannot begin to realize how frightening and real a combat vet's nightmare is. To me, there is nothing more frightening than to realize you are in a twilight sleep and you don't have the foggiest idea where you are or what year it even is. You are trying to determine whether you are dead, alive or just what. Nothing is scarier! Some of them are so frightening that I cannot remember the dream. I simply wake up terrified and soaked in sweat but I cannot remember the dream!

By the way, I never told my ex-wife of the bad dreams or waking up as described in the previous paragraph. I figured she couldn't understand them and wouldn't believe me anyway. All I did was lie in bed and grind my teeth from having bad dreams, and received elbows in the ribs to make me stop grinding my teeth.

Not all 'Nam dreams are terrifying, but when you wake up it leaves you confused, as you are trying to analyze why you had the dream(s) or what triggered it. A common non-threatening dream for me is to be in the rear area of someplace in 'Nam, preparing to come home from a second tour. I cannot remember where I had been or what I had been doing for the past year. This all stems back to the Recon platoon spending so much time in the jungle that we did have more time in the jungle than vets with two or even three tours; hence, the dream theme of the second tour. We didn't always know where we were, that was the reason for the lack of memory in the dream. That particular dream I have had hundreds of times.

A problem "awakening" I have carried for over 30 years was to suddenly wake up at 3:46 A.M. on the dot. Not a minute before or after. There were times I would wake up at exactly 3:46 A.M. two or three times a week, for reasons unknown. I would not awaken scared or in an unknown situation but I would suddenly be wide-awake. You cannot imagine the problems it has created for me through the years, like being edgy, lack of sleep when I needed it the most, and simply trying to figure out why. Why would I wake up so often at 3:46 A.M.? I had narrowed the probable field of candidates to two events, and eliminated those when it finally hit me. The first possible event was when Janae died. I thought I might have heard a noise, looked at the clock and went back to sleep, unaware of what was happening.

The second event was when I lost my "sanctuary", as mentioned later in the book. One day I was going through every significant event in my life that I could remember that could have happened in the early hours of the morning. Finally, finally it hit me. I mentioned earlier in the book about being on watch during the 'soons when it was darker than dark. I slipped going around a bush and ended up on the wrong side of a claymore mine. When I handed the watch to the next man it was 3:46 A.M.! That event has cost me more sleep than one can imagine. The mind is a mighty powerful organ, as I have mentioned numerous times. And it still wakes me at precisely 3:46 A.M. many times a month to remind me.

Being as we rarely came out of the jungle physically and especially, mentally, this has created a different type of dream. In a past dream from this influence, I was complaining to my old friend "Four Eyes" as we were preparing to head out into the bush for a mission. I was telling him that I thought the Army had regulations about having to go out in the bush after you had turned 50. This dream is because part of our thinking, or mentality, is still in the bush. Even thirty years after 'Nam we are still in the jungle mentally.

I also listed "past fears" in the context of nightmares. A past fear, nightmare, or bad dream revolves around a situation, or events that we tried to avoid or we were concerned with. A couple examples of this is having a dream or nightmare that you are preparing to go into the jungle, a combat assault, being in a firefight, or similar situation and realizing you only have three magazines of ammo. A common concern we had was making contact and running out of ammunition. Even though most of us carried 1000 rounds of ammunition, we were always concerned.

Another common nightmare is being in a situation without your weapon or being unable to find one, or one that worked. This stems from a concern we all carried about being caught off guard or our weapon jamming up. A past fear nightmare is very real and frightening, as the nightmare is from past events.

Because I was unable to openly vent my stress from 'Nam, staying in the basement or away from everyone created another problem. When I was sleeping, my internal mental stress from 'Nam was eating away at me, so I would grind my teeth in my sleep. My second wife woke me up on countless occasions because of my grinding and my jaw was sore a lot from it. Since becoming a recluse, my jaw hasn't been sore once because the grinding has decreased.

It is a tossup for me as to which dream is worst. The waking up dream where I am soaked in sweat and not knowing where I am or what year it is, is very frightening. But the times I have suddenly awaken from a bad dream where the heart is pounding 100 miles an hour and the mind has blocked remembering the dream because it was so terrifying, is just as bad.

Since 'Nam, I use a technique to reduce bad dreams. Many 'Nam vets do this also. It is called sleep deprivation. When I was married, I would stay awake as long as reasonably possible and have the alarm set early so I could reduce the number of hours I was sleeping. Sometimes it helped, and sometimes not.

Today, I still stay awake until I am almost ready to fall asleep, and then go to bed, regardless of the time.

Agent Orange is an interesting subject with many unknown side effects that will be haunting vets until the day they die (or die from it). Being as the government doesn't admit to all the defects, it makes you wonder about our group. We were in areas that had been sprayed with Agent Orange (reference back to the skull). The biggest concern all of us carried was whether our children have problems because of it.

My first daughter had severe seizure disorder supposedly resulting from having her umbilical cord around her neck during birth. This is true, except she had seizures before birth. If the cord were the real problem prior to birth, she probably would have been stillborn. This was a known problem with vets exposed to Agent Orange.

Don battled an enlarged prostate problem for three years that his doctors attributed to exposure to Agent Orange.

Howard was diagnosed with Parkinson's in late 1998. This too, has been related to Agent Orange recently.

Gary has pancreas problems, feet problems and a multitude of other problems that could be related to Agent Orange, plus back problems from the chopper going down. His heart disease has also been recently linked to Agent Orange.

Unfortunately, we won't know the full effects of our exposure to Agent Orange until it has released its full reaction on us or we are dying from it!

Hector has recently had minor eye surgery and migraine headaches.

My comments here are not blaming all the previous problems to Agent Orange. However, there are too many related issues with the five or us and Agent Orange to be purely coincidental.

If I go without socks for several hours my feet will dry up and crack open. Before I went to Vietnam, I could go barefooted for days; after I returned, my feet would dry up and sometimes bleed, until I understood what to do. This is a condition I attribute to having wet feet for weeks on end and dirty socks during the monsoons.

Don, Howard, and Hector have dead spots on their backs from carrying rucks. All of us have back problems of some sort from the rucks, as well as knee problems.

We also have other chemical concerns. I mentioned that in the monsoons, when heating water for L.R.R.P. rations we would use heating tablets and pull our poncho liner over our head to retain the heat and warm us up. These tablets were made to burn in an open area and not in a confined space. I can remember that when we didn't have enough vents in our stove, or enough air coming in under the poncho, the tablets didn't burn right, and the fumes would burn and irritate my eyes. The fumes we inhaled couldn't have been good for us.

And what happened when we did run out of heating tabs? We would use C-4 explosives to cook and warm up with. I wonder what those fumes or vapors do to you?

Another item that goes here was discussed in the hardcore section. Drinking nasty water. None of us today can drink milk. It is a condition similar to lactose intolerance but with broader problems. The correct terminology, I believe, is we have a stomach lining irritation. Drinking milk gives us upset stomachs and diarrhea. Milk turns my stomach sour in a very short period of time and the top of my stomach feels as if I had been punched there. Sometimes water also does it to me.

There are also other side effects. After places like Co Pung and quite a few combat assaults, our excitement level is different from that of most people. On a scale of 1 thru 10, and our version of a ten is Co Pung. Then everyday life is only a 1 or a 2, with today's traumas being a 3. It makes for a lot of problems in a marriage. Most women like a little excitement in their lives. Recon men have had their share of excitement and enjoy the peace and quiet. We have had enough excitement and stress to last for several more lifetimes. Four out of five of us have been divorced. Some of us twice, Only Hector has not divorced, and coincidentally, he married a lady from Thailand who had a father and an uncle serving in Vietnam. Hector also appears to be the most emotional of us, and fortunately, Hector missed going to Co Pung.

Earlier in "The Eyes Tell It All" section, I mentioned the lack of emotion aspect. That still follows us today. It goes hand in hand with the excitement level. I have grown to become a lot like "Spock" on Star Trek; the emotion level is very low. There is not much to show emotion over. It has its advantages and disadvantages. Mentally you feel almost bulletproof. You know that, in a conversation or confrontation you will be calm, and as the other person is getting upset, you are winning. It always gave me a "warm, fuzzy feeling" but unfortunately, you do not control it, it controls you! It is an addictive feeling that when pressured, comes on stronger to protect you. This goes back to the coping mechanisms of survival. Today, the only thing that has had any effect on me is visiting Janae's grave.

I did show emotion for a few minutes when my second wife left, but the mind snapped and the hardcore state immediately took over. All the pain, emotion or feelings left me, and I felt great. Look at the eyes, the faraway look got farther!

Most combat vets are normally on the defensive. Vets that were involved in small units are even more so. We are always looking around and noticing extraordinary movements. We aren't expecting the enemy to pop out from behind trees; it is involuntary and hard to stop because we don't think about doing it, or many times don't even realize we do it. Do you think about blinking your eyes? Can you make them stop? You know the answer and so do we. No, you don't think about blinking; no, you can't make them stop; and no, we can't make our involuntary movements stop either.

I read somewhere that approximately 85% of all 'Nam vets returned to lead normal or productive lives. It would be interesting to see the data. I would not dispute those numbers because I have led a productive life as well as have my good friends. I also need to interject that even though we led "productive" lives, it doesn't mean we reached our potential. Could you imagine me trying to sit in a classroom with a teacher in the front and the door in the rear? Which way would I face and how could I concentrate? Could you imagine the scene when someone would accidentally drop a book on the floor? But I am curious about the numbers. Approximately 85% is also the number of troops that were not combat troops but support troops and R.E.M.F.'s. I'm curious about the 15% that were in the combat units and about the percentage of those that are divorced and still struggle with the effects or "baggage" they carry from Vietnam.

GARY TAYLOR LETTER

*T*his letter is one I received from my closest of friends; Gary Taylor. Till the day we die we will carry a bond that cannot be explained or understood except by a few. The letter is unedited. When he refers to "finally" someone that can verify his experiences and being screwed, up he is referring to me.

Most of us were the good 'ole all American boy. Then this ugly mess came along. We didn't run or go to Canada or use a friend of the family who happened to be a politician, if this were so I wouldn't have gone because my father and the Governor of the state of Missouri were as close as two people could be; on top of all this I was a straight "A" pupil. Perfect out!!! I talked with both; the governor was a WW2 vet and fed it to me straight. I told them I did not care; this was something I must do (for some stupid reason). So it's basic, infantry AIT, jump school, some time with the Green Berets then to Germany. They found out I was a sole surviving son. Finally orders to 'Nam after a lot of negotiating. I have now racked up about 3 months of jungle warfare training. Next is Recon. (Here I jump around a bit as things come to mind). The problem is this; The U.S. Government made us what we were. They had what they wanted. A platoon of perfectly willing and capable killers. I found this out in less than 30 days. I'd no qualms what ever of pulling the trigger. Later it hit me I just killed someone, what the hell; that was our job wasn't it? What the U.S. government did was invent what they wanted and boy did they get their moneys worth. However they forgot to install one important thing, an off switch. So in many cases such as mine, the switch never goes off and the battery keeps going. I will never say that any of this was done to me without my own knowledge. I knew every step of that what was going on. I could have quit but I didn't. However I did not know that after 30 years I'd be just like I was then. Again no ones fault.

You come home, if that's what you and everyone and everything has changed. What happened to these people, are they crazy? I don't know who they are and worst of all I don't trust anyone, including family. I tell no one a thing and live with it until I can't stand it anymore. So I seek sanctuary. The people in the Army want me to return. They offer me a job. I say "no" and in two years I'm back in S.E. Asia. It's still not as rough as the first one but I still <u>trust no one.</u> I stay this was until I find ……. Finally someone who verifies what I am saying, everyone else thinks I've made all this up. I believe I've made it up. I think I am crazy. Then it hits me, for almost 30 years I've been living in a fog not knowing who I am or what I am and right from wrong. I find he is the same way. I can tell from the moment I see him. Ya! He's screwed up too, even though he might not realize it and if he does he doesn't want to admit it to himself.

I found out many things people don't want to associate with me cause they think I'm nuts. Even other 'Nam vets stay away from me. Why? I'm always polite and smile a lot. But it's the eyes, no ones home. Fine with me I don't like people anyway. I keep conversation short and on general subjects. I've done what I was trained to do. Control the course of events. Listen, sort it out, discharge the unimportant and read between the lines. It can keep you alive.

I've heard many people say 'Nam was about personal survival. Not for us. It was about family survival. We weren't a unit. We were a family, a family that was closer than any family you could be born into. If a man got hurt or killed it was like watching a parent die and not a damn thing you can do but to stand by and watch. I have seen both parents die and after a year or so its over with. You remember them but you don't sit around and pine about it. If one of us went down 30 years later you still remember. You cry, you don't like to admit it but you do. You keep wandering what you should have done to change it. It all sounds so good to you, but; that isn't the way it happened.

As for myself I keep to myself. No one knows much about me cause I don't tell them. I don't want friends and I go out of my way not to make any. I know almost everyone in this small town but no one really knows me. I like it that way.

AND NOW...THE FACTS AND PAYING THE PRICE

*A*uthor's note: *This chapter was written in a manner to reflect a series of thoughts and events, and the details may not be in chronological order.*

And now, where do I start? This portion of the book is a reflection of the past several months and past 30 plus years. After rereading this book and reflecting on the past, many things have come into focus and are clearer than ever. After reading Gary's letter, the first obvious fact is that I'm screwed up and didn't want to admit it. That's the hard part, openly admitting after all those years that you had a problem and tried to conceal it and not deal with it. And before you judge my denial too harshly, how many times have you had a problem and not openly admitted it or dealt with it in a timely manner? I am not that different than anyone else.

Early in this book, where I refer to friends and nicknames, I came across a problem or realization of a situation. I did not mention that I was "Lambchops" as referred to in the past tense; I said I <u>am</u> "Lambchops". This struck me as odd at first, then I realized that on the cover page I wrote Richard Price, and in the end I signed it as Richard "Lambchops" Price. To me, this indicated that I have basically completed the regression back to the mental state of when I was in 'Nam. I can thank being hardcore and P.T.S.D. for this, or as Gary stated, we didn't have an off switch installed. In looking back there are other signals or events that helped "Lambchops" to become the obvious dominant side and resurface.

When I came across Gary, Howie, Don, and Hector the war stories came alive again because I could tell them to someone that was there and a lot of memories resurfaced. Even "Wild Bill" didn't remember my name but instantly knew me when I said "Lambchops". When we met a couple of times to eat and reminisce, we referred to each other by our nicknames.

So, what does this all mean? Depends upon how you look at it. The "Lambchops" portion or altered state of mind has been with me since 'Nam and will be with me until the day I die. In the past, it was more dormant than dominant. It has always been there ready to surface and take over. Many of the attitudes and characteristics have controlled me but not as strongly as now. When we were in 'Nam we learned to survive and had to become hardcore, as talked about throughout the book. It was time for me to take the time to cope with my past, and in order to do that the "Lambchops" side of me had to come out and become dominant, for it was again time to survive. But again, I am no different than the average person. When you encounter difficult times or situations, what do you do? You go back to past experiences or skills to help you through your problem.

And what did I do to survive and cope? I quit! I fully quit the world. Being as society and most of the world gave up on us, I gave up on the world. It was my turn!

On September 11th of 2000, I gave my two weeks notice and said I was retiring. It all sounded great and everyone bought it. I didn't really retire though. I believe the correct term is, I ran. I knew I had to get out of Indiana, away from two ex-wives, and take care of myself. On September 22nd, which was also my 51st birthday, I quit work and started quitting the world. Two days later, I arrived in southern Colorado to start working full time on myself. The reason I say full time is because as I reflect back, I have always struggled since I returned from 'Nam. Every house I have lived in and every job I have had always had a place of sanctuary in it.

Sanctuary is an interesting term or thought. Amazingly, my good friend Gary and I were talking one day, and he referred to seeking sanctuary and getting away from everyone. He even mentions this in his letter. Because of our experiences together in 'Nam, we are similar in so many ways. Even though we had been out of contact for 27 ½ years, we both used the term sanctuary as a place to escape to so we could cope with the past.

I never realized how badly I struggled until I got away from it all and came to the mountains of Colorado. As I look back, I was always trying to cope or escape by going to my sanctuary. I wonder how much of my life since 'Nam has been lost by being in a place of sanctuary. I know in my last marriage to my second "wife" I spent countless days or weekends in the basement trying to allow myself some room to cope. If it wasn't the basement in the winter, it was the woods in the summer, or getting on my bicycle and peddling to wherever.

When I would go into sanctuary, one of two things would happen. Either I would try to occupy my time with the computer, television, or reading, or I would sit with the deep stare in my eyes. The older I got the more I would have the 1000-yard stare or "space out". The eyes tell it all! Often, I would simply sit in front of the fire and be mentally paralyzed, just sitting there. Frozen in time and unable to get up. I would sit for hours. When I would come out of it, I didn't know the time or what had been on television. This was a common thing I would and still do.

I can remember numerous occasions when I was sitting somewhere and someone would ask me what I was staring at or if I would quit staring at them because it was making them uncomfortable. What they didn't realize or see, was the faraway look in the eyes. I wasn't staring, but spacing out. It happened at home, with the kids or at ballparks while waiting for a ballgame to start.

Even at work I would sometimes space out in some form. Normally, at lunch I would turn out the lights in my office, lock the door and prop my feet up on my desk. A blank look would enter my eyes and I would think about nothing, or whatever I was thinking about was forgotten. I always told people when they came in my office that I was thinking about a problem pertaining to work. I have always been sharp enough or smart enough that I could think of some quick answer to a problem and people were impressed by the answer. Typically, I had figured it out earlier in the day, and when they interrupted my spacing out, I really wasn't home!

A little simple math helps put the coping time into perspective. I probably averaged a minimum of one day a week (total) in sanctuary in one form or another. That means 52 days a year, or 1560 days over the past 30 years, or about 4 ¼ years. That is a lot of time spent escaping reality and coping with the past. In the later years before moving to Colorado, I would spend one to two weeks annually in Colorado, in the middle of nowhere, to try and cope for an extended period so I could make it a little longer. The solo vacations started in 1993 and were a signal that I was going downhill, or the "Lambchops" side of me was starting to become more dominant. I just didn't recognize the signs. The trips to Colorado were in an isolated area where I was out of communications with the world. A preview of what was to come.

But the 1993 slide was really a continuation of the on-going slide I was in. After some deep reflecting of the past and sorting out the pieces, I realized that the slide started at the end of 1978. I had been physically out of 'Nam for about 7 years and trying to lead a somewhat normal life, considering the difficult circumstances. Janae had been struggling through the past 2-½ years with brain damage and seizure disorder. I had always quietly placed the blame on myself because of exposure to Agent Orange. It was a guilt trip I carried because I knew of the possible association. I never discussed it with anyone and kept it buried, along with other problems associated with 'Nam. When she passed away on the Sunday morning of December 31, 1978, I mourned very deeply and took it very personally because of the possible association with Agent Orange. To cope with the situation, I reverted back to the hardcore state of mind. It was still fresh in me and it started taking over. And remember, it possesses you. I turned colder to my wife and friends. Fortunately, my job entailed working with one other person, with whom I was a friend, so it didn't affect my work.

The signs were there that I was sliding, but no one, including myself, saw them. The slide sustained itself slowly. In 1983, I bought a piece of property to build a house on. For the area I lived in, it was considered "removed" from the normal world. It was off the road a ways and in the middle of a large woods. I started building an underground house. It was my first attempt at building a sanctuary, getting away, and shutting myself off from the world. It was physically demanding and wore me out, as I worked on the house 50 to 60 hours a week plus worked a full time job. Mentally, it was helping because I knew the end result of getting farther away from society was drawing nearer.

During the project, my wife and I had another daughter who was perfectly healthy. We were both hoping that having Erin would help save the relationship, but obviously it didn't. As the project progressed, my wife informed me that she was divorcing me. Then in 1987, I received a phone call from the police department that my sanctuary had burnt to the ground. Another major stumbling block, or hurdle thrown at me, and the slide continued on. Most people grow from experiences in some form or another, but because of my 'Nam experience, my coping mechanism was to return to being even more hardcore and it had all the reasons to revert back and take over. At that point in my life I should have thrown up my hands and quit, but I didn't. It was a major mistake, not quitting then, but it is a bigger mistake to dwell on it.

I did remarry in an attempt to stabilize the condition, or myself, but to make a long story short, it didn't work and I was divorced in 1999. The slide at that point started a deep, downhill spiral that didn't stop until I quit the world. And here I am, trying to cope with it after 30 years.

Coping, going to sanctuary, the 1000-yard stare, or spacing out is common to a lot of 'Nam vets. I never took time to cope with my problem because I was too macho or had too large an ego to admit it and I just couldn't see it. In the previous chapter, Gary's letter mentioned that he knew I was screwed up as soon as he saw me, and he was right! He even mentioned that I didn't realize it or didn't want to admit it, and he hit a bull's eye.

Now I am finally taking the time to cope, and to do that, I quit the world. I gave my mother my television and several other pieces of furniture before I left Indiana, in early September of 2000. Other than watching a movie on the VCR, I haven't turned the tube on since September of 2000, and I haven't bought a newspaper since November of 2000. I gave up listening to radio years earlier because of the many commercials. I don't miss the news, or typically, the bad news of the day, nor do I miss all the garbage and commercials. As I said, I gave up on the world. I refused to be a part of it.

When I left Indiana, I walked away from my house. I had never missed a payment in over 39 years on anything, but when I arrived in Colorado I called the bank and told them they could have it. We finished exchanging the paperwork in July of 2001. It was irrelevant to me because I also would get nothing out of the house if I did sell it. Before I left Indiana, the bank had offered to max out my credit line to pay off my ex-wife, so I did (pay off the ex), and left.

SERVING OUR COUNTRY AND PAYING THE PRICE

As I sit here, typing these unorganized sets of paragraphs, I am finally at peace with myself. I enjoy the solitude and quiet of the mountains. I am currently living in a one-bedroom log cabin in southern Colorado that I designed and built. I was without running water for approximately 8 weeks, and lived off my temporary electrical setup with extension cords for about 6 weeks, but I am happy here. For the first time in 30 years, I am in a place that I can honestly say I am happy in. I have cut myself off from the world as much as possible. No television, no radio, no newspaper, almost no neighbors to contend with, only a cellular telephone (which is never turned on because I hate to hear it ring), and no Internet. I do make trips into town about once a week for supplies, and I make regular trips into Pueblo to the V.A.

As you can tell from the previous paragraphs, I have finally accomplished what I started out to do over 18 years ago.

When going to Pueblo I am mentally on high alert; too many people and too much civilization and society. I go there to the V.A. to see Bev, my therapist, and that helps me sort out the pieces of the puzzle. It also makes me think more and sometimes I over-analyze things too much, which aggravates her occasionally, but that's okay. It has started the ball rolling for 100% disability status (more on that in a moment).

As I discuss disability status, Social Security recently approved my claim for disability. After about 35 minutes into the interview, the psychologist for Social Security decided he had heard enough for the claim. He commented, based upon the reports from the V.A. and my comments, that I had chronic P.T.S.D. I think my response was something like "no kidding"; so what does that translate to for my claim? His next comments somewhat surprised me because I do not like being labeled. He informed me that he did not want me to be in the work force ever again. He explained to me that I was considered a threat or endangerment to the work force. He was concerned that if I got upset, people might disappear. He basically stated that if I stayed in the mountains and left people alone, I would receive Social Security benefits.

I was taken back, but he was also positive about his approach. He stated that I had done everything right as far as removing myself from society and setting myself up in the mountains, and preferred that I stayed in the mountains. The thing I appreciated was, on the way out he said, "welcome home" and wished me luck. I haven't seen the official report but the paperwork I received stated that, by their standards, I was considered disabled on September 22, 2000, my last day of work. That in itself is unusual, but upon a visit to the Social Security office in town to clear up some details, I was informed that instead of the customary reviews for my status I would be sent paperwork in the mail, in 3 years, to fill out. And they didn't want to see me any more. Interesting, considering all the war stories I've heard about Social Security.

At this point, you probably are wondering why the psychiatrist from Social Security was so concerned about me working again and being around people. First of all, he had read all the reports from the V.A. on me. Some of Bev's comments were worse than his thoughts. Some of the answers I gave him in the interview firmed up his concerns. Why would he be concerned that people would disappear? Because I had admitted that, in certain situations in the past, I had planned to take what I felt was appropriate action against individuals to reduce the threat or problem they were imposing. This was going to happen by them having accidents of some type or by m.a's (mechanical ambushes) of some form. But keep in mind that in conversation with the others in the Recon group, they had all planned similar scenarios because of situations they were involved in. And you have to remember our experience and actions. As mentioned in several places in the book, we always initiated the contact and left. Then disappeared in the bush as if nothing had happened.

He had or has every right to be concerned, because I still catch myself thinking that way on occasions. Now to keep things in the proper perspective, you must remember our extremely strong will to survive. Being they (the N.V.A.) couldn't get us in 'Nam, anyone posing what we perceived to be a threat is considered the enemy, and with the enemy, we took appropriate action. A reckless or drunk driver, or anyone making physical or verbal threats could be perceived as the enemy.

Another comment on disabilities. I received a copy of my claim from the law firm handling my V.A. disability case. In reviewing the evidence, I noticed that all the information or documents were the ones I had sent in or Gary had sent verifying my statement on Co Pung. I asked the researcher if she had received any information on me from the government. She had received my medical records from the V.A., but I can also do that with a phone call. And interestingly enough, they did not receive any information on me from the government. Another interesting detail of my V.A. claim, was the request for my Social Security report showing my disability and details thereof. The first response from Social Security was, my files had been archived. Interesting that my file had been placed in deep storage less than a month after it was approved. The second request came back with more confusing explanations. My file was archived, lost, but also unavailable for public review! Why?

Also, when I was reviewing my records to send to the law firm, I noticed numerous discrepancies. For example, I was discharged under a different social security number according to my records (supposedly an error). My DD-214 shows my unit, as "F" Company, not Echo Company. Foxtrot Company only existed in the minds of "Wild Bill" and I as we were playing mind games with the enemy. The documents showing me going to the Recon platoon had the wrong dates on them, and I also have copies of orders showing I was assigned to Headquarters Company, which I never was in.

I should inject at this point the details and results of my V.A. claim. The psychiatrist doing the Compensation and Pension review explained to me that the exam and report would take two hours to complete. The exam itself lasted two hours. My therapist explained that the normal report would be two to three pages in length; mine was 6 pages. The psychiatrist stated in his report that the evidence was "significant" for the case. The evidence submitted was this chapter of the book, less this portion, and included some of the records I had from my days in 'Nam. I also need to add here that approximately 2 ½ months prior to my C&P exam, I received a letter from the V.A.. It indicated they had received an "informal" claim (which infuriated the law firm), with uncertified copies of my DD-214, Air Medal, Gary's form 2-1 and a "buddy statement" from Gary stating we were in 'Nam together and on Co Pung. Everything was listed as uncertified, and they would request the information so it would be certifiable. And true to what I had been told, the psychiatrist admitted that "they" could not obtain any information on me during my days in 'Nam. The psychiatrist did have information on me from Basic Training and Advanced Individual Training, and nothing else.

Twenty-six days after the C&P exam, my claim was approved with no questions asked. Total time from the date the claim was filed, was 7 months. Not a record, but it was one of the quickest claims the law firm could remember. And I was classified as 100% permanently disabled the first time through, and again, no questions. Kind of makes you wonder, doesn't it? Social Security makes my records unavailable, the V.A. was unable to obtain any information or proof I was in 'Nam other than my DD-214 showing my Combat Infantryman's Badge. Remember that my DD-214 was incorrect; it showed Company "F". My statements were not questioned nor was any information I had submitted. Gary's "buddy statement" referencing Co Pung was listed as verifying my stressor (this chapter), and that is it! I expected more of a fight considering they classed all my evidence as uncertified!

As I planned and laid out my information for the law firm, I approached it as if I were going into a courtroom for a lawsuit. I figured that I had to prove my case, and expected them to challenge information or statements because the information has been unattainable. There was not any discrepancy of my P.T.S.D., being as it is well documented. Instead, they basically rolled over and pleaded "no contest". It is a fairly bold statement for the V.A. to accept all my future medical costs and pay me a disability solely on my evidence! Not knowing how their computer system works and information available, I would have to speculate that red flags started popping up when the Recon unit or my name was entered in to verify my service time. I state this because; if something of this nature wasn't true, why no questions or hassles?

So with all the comments made referencing my disability, what does all this mean? Pretty simple to figure out. It all goes back to the time in 'Nam. In the jungle, we didn't have links to the outside world nor did we care. We were in a situation that required all of our faculties to survive. That is what is going on today, and that is why the "Lambchops" side of me is so dominant today. I am in a mode of survival and going back to the hardest of the hardcore state is what allows me to do this. Even though I was quite unemotional and hardcore before, I returned to the full state of hardcore and no emotion; so most of life becomes painless. Leaving Indiana, old friends, a house, reality, holidays, and a good income was all painless and without feelings. This makes coping easier, but also creates possibly a larger problem. I have mentioned numerous times through the book that I wouldn't want to return to normal or live without being hardcore. I've also mentioned that the hardcore state controls or dominates you. That combination creates a set of problems that is very difficult to overcome. How do you convince the brain that it is time to return to a state of feeling emotion and pain, which is just the opposite of what it wants?

Actually, this whole situation I am in now is what I needed, in my opinion. First of all, I am in my sanctuary and I am in it almost 24 hours a day, 7 days a week. My cabin and the mountains are my sanctuary. Without the world to contend with, coping becomes easier to work on. When I was in the Midwest, I was always taking care of everyone else's problems, and with all that behind me and out of the way, I am at last in a place where I can start to cope and put some of the pieces in place. As I wrote earlier in the book, I (we, the 'Nam vets) can only cope, as there are too many broken parts and too many missing pieces or voids to fill. I know that I will never be okay as society looks at me, but being as I don't carry the emotional portion of the brain, it is absolutely irrelevant to me. All I want to do is to be left alone, be a recluse, and spend time with a few select friends, attempting to cope with the situation and make the best of it.

I have pretty much taken what I call the "Forrest Gump" approach to life. When he was sitting at the bus stop and explaining to a lady about his running across the U.S., he commented that: when he was hungry he ate; when he was tired he slept; and when he had to "you know what", well he went. That is my approach to life now.

Typically, I call my good friend "Four Eyes" on a regular basis as well as "Pappy", "Wild Bill", and "Marty". We often tell the same war stories over and over again, and at some point in the conversation, we almost always talk about Co Pung or other situations in 'Nam. It's not that we are reliving it; it is how we are coping. For almost 28 years we didn't talk about it and we have a lot of catching up to do. As I am writing this particular section, tomorrow is April 30, 2001, the 30th anniversary of Co Pung. Gary and I talked about it yesterday, there are so many questions still unanswered with us and we cannot remember it all. A short comment that sums up the experience of 'Nam and

Co Pung: _The impact 'Nam had on us was unforgettable but the impact Co Pung had on us is unimaginable._

Everyone has stories or events that you talk about when reminiscing with old friends. Some events were good, and some were bad, but you don't talk about the same event in some form in every conversation you have with your old friends. The impact, outcome, and questions regarding Co Pung threw us in a mental warp that we will never get out of, and this is the only way we can cope with it. You have to remember that we were sent in to be eliminated. We were red-lined before we hit the ground, and Gary's helicopter was shot down. We can never forget it. Surprisingly, I am happy to celebrate the anniversary. I say that because I made it back, and too many didn't. And for those that didn't, may they rest in peace!

As I talk about Gary, many things need to be explained. First of all, he was the first person in 27 ½- years that believed what I said about 'Nam and vice versa. Because no one believed us, we didn't talk about it. We both had lived in a fog for 27 ½- years until we reunited. But because of what we experienced together in 'Nam: the sleeping back to back during the monsoons to keep warm; 50 plus combat assaults together; Co Pung mountain; being listed as killed in action twice together; the trust we had in each other (and remember, we don't trust anyone); excessive time in the jungle; extremely hardcore; and on and on. What we have isn't friendship as defined in the dictionary. It goes far beyond that. It goes beyond bonding and being brothers, or of being family. It even goes deeper than the soul. I know that at some point in the future, we all will depart this earth. And when one of us goes, the other will feel an empty place in him that cannot be explained or replaced. After the life and death situations we were in and knowing unequivocally that we could trust each other, knowing we have been to Hell and back together and did more or saw more than God had ever intended on us seeing or doing, words don't really explain our relationship. Outside of having my two daughters and quitting the world, reuniting with Gary, Howard, Don and Hector was undoubtedly the most significant event in my life in the last 30 years.

There are always questions that can't be answered, but I have often pondered what "Four Eyes", "Wild Bill", "Pappy", "Marty" and I would be like if we had not reunited. I know that we have helped each other tremendously because we believe each other. We can at least talk about what we went through instead of holding it in and being in a fog. I cannot imagine how much deeper in the hole any of us would be if we had not reunited.

Here are the facts of who we are, or were, as I know them to be. Being I am reasonably good with math, one plus one is supposed to equal two. Many things I have found or been told add up; some don't. I am going to attempt to list different facts or details and explain the best I can of who we were.

I cannot overemphasize that, in the end results, it is all very irrelevant or meaningless whom we worked for because it does not change a single detail or second of what we went through. The facts of who we were; the Recon platoon, 2/502 of the 101st Airborne Division was really a black operations group set up by the Department of ********* and our wages were even paid for by them. Technically, when we were in the Recon platoon we weren't in the Army. We were part of the Second Special Operations Group or 2nd SOG unit. Our orders came from the CIA and other intelligence groups, and probably funneled through the Brigade to the Battalion Commander during my tour. There are no attainable records on us, so we didn't exist. Most probably, the assault we led on Co Pung was a planned attempt to have us wiped out. It was also an operation controlled by the CIA. But we fooled them all by surviving the assault and they had to send in reinforcements. Having us wiped out would end any trails showing we ever existed. No survivors, no history, no proof! The N.V.A lost approximately 650 killed or wounded from the Co Pung assault. I assume that was mainly from air strikes and artillery.

As I have mentioned throughout this book, being a Recon man was being one of the elite. To help define how elite Recon was, I obtained the following information. There were three units set up by a Department in the Government. Two were in the Army and one in the Marines. Approximately 300 to 400 of the 3,100,000 men that went to 'Nam were chosen for the three units. So being in the Recon platoon was indeed a privilege. It was also a very high-risk unit. It is estimated that approximately 100 or so of us made it back! Recon, 2/502 was the last operating unit. The Marine unit was basically wiped out and the other Army unit suffered very heavy casualties, and ceased to function as well. Most likely, Co Pung was the last "Recon" operation as it was organized in those days. Which means "Wild Bill" and I closed the chapter on Recon, as we were the last two off of Co Pung. After Co Pung we were just marking time because we did not have a function or true mission plan, because we were not supposed to come off Co Pung. Remember that we were "red-lined" when we took off on the assault.

I truly do not believe anyone in the Recon platoon and "Echo" company knew of our organizational arrangement. I think the Battalion or Brigade Commander is where the chain of knowledge possibly started. No one in Recon was ever told it was a "black" unit because we didn't need to know. At least, that was the opinion of our employer. Being as we were never around other troops in the bush and only around troops during a standdown period, which was rare, the secret was easy to maintain.

Now with all of that being said, the question of verification of this information comes up. When I submitted my documentation to the law firm handling my V.A. claim, part of what I submitted were copies of orders connecting "Wild Bill", "Pappy", "Marty", "Four Eyes" and I together in 'Nam. That way any of the four could send verifying documents. "Four Eyes" sent a statement saying he served with me in 'Nam and we were on Co Pung together, and a copy of his form 2-1. I also sent many different copies of original records I had. This included documents with conflicting information on them concerning dates and units. This was an effort to show the V.A. that my records might have problems. The V.A. referenced this information as unverified documents and swept them aside as dust in the wind. So everything submitted to the law firm was basically null and void...except for one document. A signed affidavit by an independent, outside party was submitted on my behalf to the law firm handling my case. This affidavit was to be used for my case only, and the agreement stated that it could be shown only to the V.A, nobody else. The affidavit states or admits that Recon 2/502 was a black operations unit, in fact a SOG unit, primarily under control of the CIA and other intelligence groups. This individual used to work for the people that set up the structure of the Recon platoon, so the information is accurate.

When I was searching on the Internet for fellow Recon survivors, I came across anything and everything. Except for other vets trying to find others in Recon, there was nothing on Recon 2/502. I found quite a bit of information on SOG (special operation groups), which was a volunteer unit similar to ours. There were even ads for commemorative handguns and knives for them, but nothing on Recon 2/502.

Before I left Indiana, I met an ex Army Captain that had worked in the Phoenix program. He had worked with SOG units when in 'Nam and was aware they had two "units". As we were discussing my unit and the information I had obtained, he was quite sure we were part of the 2nd SOG unit.

I also mentioned earlier in the chapter that the V.A. had no information on me during my tenure in 'Nam. I was told by an individual in the V.A. that the interviewer for my C&P exam did not have the clearance to see my records. As a matter of fact, the individual stated that they did not have the clearance to see my records, nor did anyone else in the whole V.A. system, except for <u>one</u> person. If only one person in the whole V.A. system has access to my records, what does that tell you? That individual also stated that I was in a black unit because my time in 'Nam had to be verified by this one individual with a high enough security clearance. And remember, this is coming from the Veterans Administration that Recon was a black unit!

After I received my V.A. disability, I received a letter from Social Security that I was receiving back pay because I was being credited with a second year of military service. Being as Social Security had access to all my work records, this means there was a flag of some sort in the system or a blank space indicating a special approval was needed in this situation. So why was it not listed?

We didn't do anything that would be considered classified today. So why can't we find anything on us? I don't believe that it was our missions, even though I believe it was possible we were slipped into Laos a couple of times, and because of Co Pung (An Dong Vong). And I believe the last sentence because, as I have mentioned earlier, many times we were out of radio range or close to it, as well as being out of artillery range. I have to believe it was the decision and reporting structure relating to Recon, or in other terms, who subcontracted us.

It is also appropriate to mention that I know that we weren't the only "black" unit. I know of Marines and other Army vets that also served in units that were "black". The only difference is, they knew it was a "black" unit and they volunteered for it

And paying the price... How do you place a price or value on what we lost in 'Nam? Even defining what we lost is hard to find words for. Mathematically, it would be a very long and complicated equation and in the end, it would not add up or make sense. Being screwed up and living in a fog is only part of the equation.

People often think of 'Nam vets as individuals that use their past as an excuse for acting the way they do. I am sure that there are a few cases where this is true, but not very often. My ex-wife thought so, as well as millions of other Americans. Most of these people don't think we lost much, if anything at all, because they have no clue as to what we experienced or went through. Let me list some of the things that I've lost due to 'Nam, or possibly related to, and see if anyone can place a value on it.

First on the list has to be the lack of emotion and handling stress. So many people I have met through the years think it is wonderful to be able to shrug off stress or anything else the way I do. I have talked to many people who think that the low state of emotion I possess is admirable and very desirable. I know of several people that wish they could borrow my lack of emotion attitude for a few months because of problems in relationships, or just having a rough time of things. First of all, it possesses you, you do not possess it. It is part of the package deal from being hardcore. There have been many times in my life when I wished I could wave some magic wand and return to normal, with emotions like everyone else, but as I said, it possesses you. If a window of opportunity opened to throw out the lack of emotion attitude, it would close the window before you realized it was open. Like I said; it possesses you.

My level of emotion is very even and unwavering, unless I feel I am threatened. Then I quietly become excited and very defensive, and then start evaluating or figuring out ways to eliminate the threat, without any outward signs. The look in the eyes just becomes deeper! That is why my therapist and the psychiatrist from Social Security were so concerned about my actions and considered me a threat. And stress? After being shot at so many times, and places like Co Pung, my opinion of stress as known by most people today is, it doesn't exist. On a scale of 1 to 10, with Co Pung being a 10, today's problems rate only a 1 or 2 on my scale. I know the lack of emotion played a major role in both my divorces, more so on the second than the first. My first divorce would have happened sooner or later from problems growing out of Janae's death, and because of my hardcore state of mind.

Janae.... I'll never know if her seizure disorder was a by-product of my exposure to Agent Orange. She paid a terrible price if it was. And if it was, how do you place a price on the loss of a child? Sometimes I do not know what is worse, losing a child or not knowing if it was my fault because I was serving my Country. I carry a small amount of survivor's guilt from time to time because of the situations we were in, but too many times I blame myself for Janae's problems because I know I was exposed to Agent Orange. If the two are related, that is one hell of a price to pay for serving your Country.

No emotion, two divorces, and one lost child. Is the price adding up yet? Let me add some more to it.

How about simple things like eating in a restaurant and being fully relaxed. I can't do it. Once I have been properly seated so my back is not towards the door, and normally in a corner or off to the side, I am on full alert and watching every person walk by me, trying to determine if they are a threat. Even the waitress walking by causes me to take a defensive posture. I'm not being curious of people going by or nosey, but it is instinct to be on defense. It goes back to the mindset that we trusted no one, other than our closest friends in the unit and ourselves.

There is another one: being on defense. Do you have any idea what it is like to be always looking around to make sure you will be okay? Almost any little movement triggers the brain to kick into gear to determine if there is a problem or a threat, and what countermeasures need to be taken. This includes anything from shadows moving, to birds flying by, to seeing someone walk down the same side of the street you are on. Now you might understand why I don't like crowds or being around people. Do we have a total price or figure yet?

How about tinitus? How can I ever forget 'Nam when my ears ring 24 hours a day 7, days a week. As I was always on the first helicopter in, the M-60's always opened up when it was "show time" and my hearing was damaged because of it.

How about a good night's sleep? In the mountains, as a recluse, I am sleeping better but I do not sleep deeply. I don't wake up when the refrigerator kicks on but I am subconsciously aware of it. If the house creaks differently, or the wood in the stove pops differently, I am wide-awake. It is better than

Indiana because I am removed from the population and most threats. When I lived alone, I had to chain and padlock my bedroom door nightly.

As we are thinking of sleep, how about dreams? My brother and I have talked about dreams on numerous occasions and how he tries to remember his dreams. I have no desire to have dreams, let alone trying to remember them. The majority of times, when I go to bed, I have tried to stay awake as long as I can so I fall immediately to sleep, and hopefully I don't dream, or I dream very little. You cannot imagine what it is like to wake up wringing wet in the middle of the night, trying to figure out if it is 1971 or 2001, and you have no idea where you are. Thank goodness for my alarm clock with large L.E.D.'s that is able to help snap me back to reality. As I reflect back on my sleep habits, even in Indiana I would stay up late and set the alarm early to reduce the amount of sleep I was getting (sleep deprivation), hoping to reduce dreamtime. Are you still adding or calculating the price?

Flashbacks fit into place here. A recent flashback was when I was driving down a mountain road at night and the recently fallen snow had melted and puddled along the side of the road. It was windy, and I was driving with my brights on. The reflection of the lights hit the puddle just right, scattering and fragmenting the light. It gave an instantaneous image of an explosion similar to a mortar hitting. I hit the brakes and slowed down quickly, but it took the next mile or two to recompose myself, and all I could say was damn, damn, damn, damn and grit my teeth. Still adding?

How about P.T.S.D.? That short set of abbreviations carries a lot of elements. Look in the eyes and nobody is home. Jumping because of a pop or some noise that triggered your defense mechanisms. Going to sanctuary because it is time to take a time out to try and cope for a few minutes. So many things are related to P.T.S.D. that are hard to list. Still calculating?

Here is the hardest one to place a value on. After a lost child, two divorces, lost emotion, nobody home, being very hardcore, P.T.S.D, what can be worse?

I lost myself!

I am not me. If you could place me next to myself when I was in high school or before I went into the service, would I recognize myself?

No!

I would like to turn back the mental clock and become the person I was at 19. Being fifty-one years old is not a big deal, but it would be nice to be able to be carefree in regards to emotion. To be able to be excited because you are going on a date or vacation, or feeling hurt for a week or two, or even being able to shed a tear because your girl friend dumped you. To be eating in a restaurant and be completely oblivious to anything that is going on around you. If I looked at that person I would swear it was someone else instead of me. One cannot imagine what it is like to lose yourself. The original me is gone forever. Part of that person was lost on the first night in the jungle, some was lost in the first fire fight. Daily, shreds of me were lost in the jungle as we were surviving. Every time we heard incoming rounds headed our way, a part of me was lost. Part of the original me was washed out during the monsoons and the cold, and sweated out in the summer heat. Part of the original me fell to the ground whenever I threw the 120-pound ruck on my back and humped. Bits and pieces of the original me were ripped off and scattered through Vietnam every time we had a combat assault. What was left of the original me was lost or decimated on Co Pung. Today, there is only a shell of the original me. If you looked at pictures of me prior to 'Nam, and compared them to pictures after, you could see it in my eyes. The twinkle in my eyes was driven out by the monsoons and combat assaults; now there is only emptiness that goes to the spot where my soul use to be. It was also lost somewhere in the jungle or mountains.

How do I find the original me? I never will because the original me is lost forever, in places I can never find and places I never want to return to.

With so many pieces missing, you cannot put together a whole person. As I reflect back, I believe this is why I removed myself from society and why Gary has done the same thing, except not to the extreme I went to. We are both very intelligent individuals; that was the reason we were handpicked for the Recon platoon. We both realized we couldn't function properly in the world, and that when we tried to fit in, we struggled badly. He simply realized it or admitted it long before I did.

In our conversations, we both realized we had regressed to the state of minds we had in 'Nam. And regressed is probably the wrong term for where we are. To regress means we had to go forward first. We never left that spot, or progressed past that point. We made a lateral movement to a different position, letting people think we had progressed passed that point. But that was part of the survival technique we used in 'Nam; tell everyone including the enemy we moved, when we hadn't. For the past 30 years we have been doing the same thing mentally; fooling everyone including ourselves into believing we have moved on, but we never have. We may be physically located in the U.S.A., but our mental state is still in the bush or up on Co Pung. To make a long story short, we are still in the jungle. We never left 'Nam and we return daily.

I need to interject another point or comment for all this to make sense. In Gary's letter, he mentioned controlling the course of events. In 'Nam we controlled the course of events as much as possible. We couldn't do much about the combat assaults, but otherwise we controlled, within our limits, the course of events. When contact was initiated with the N.V.A. it was <u>always</u> our decision, not theirs. Our ability to survive in the jungle and stay undetected was based upon our control of the situation(s): whispering, moving quietly, etc. After 'Nam, it was the same thing.

Gary was in a position where he needed to be in control of the situation and so was I. In my management position several years ago, I took a personality test to determine what I was strongest in. Mine was being in control; any surprise? My graph was also the most radical in the company. It showed that I needed to be in control, work in small groups, and be left alone. Being in control has always been a strong point or necessity for me, which also created problems in the marriage.

Being in control is the reason why we go to sanctuary or remove ourselves from society. We are fine when we are in control of ourselves, the environment, P.T.S.D., and any other surroundings. It is when we lose control or get out of control that the problems arise. I believe we are intelligent enough to control the course of events and stay out of that situation. The proof of that is obvious; I'm in the mountains of Colorado and Gary is in sanctuary a lot. The less contact we have with society, the more we can control the situation or environment. I honestly believe that if either of us lost our sanctuary or was forced to go back into the world, it would drive us crazy or kill us, literally.

For the last statement to be understood, you need to think of the last time you were driving down a busy road during rush hour traffic and a squirrel attempted to dart across the road. His head was moving back and forth frantically and his eyes were darting to and fro, trying to pick a path across the road between cars. Inevitably, he was run over. There were too many cars to watch for. Squirrels are fine in the country, where there is more space, less traffic, and smaller country roads. His chances for survival are greatly increased.

Vets with severe P.T.S.D. in society are somewhat like the squirrel in traffic; they don't belong there. That is why we like the solitude or space. Squirrels don't belong in rush hour traffic and we don't belong in the rush hour of society.

To help define severe P.T.S.D. as it relates to us, a rating is given by the therapist indicating the level or severity of the P.T.S.D. This is called a GAF (global axis functioning) rating, based upon a possible score of 100. As I understand the ratings, commonly vets with 100% disability score below 70. My rating is 40. According to the law firm that handled my V.A. claim, that of the hundreds of cases they have handled, possibly one claimant had a lower score than mine. Gary's initial score was 26. It is the lowest his therapist has given or seen. I don't think it takes a rocket scientist to figure out that these two extremely low scores indicate how much effect our jungle time and Co Pung had on us. According to my therapist, Gary and I hold the unique distinction of being the only two 'Nam vets she has heard of that served together and can combine their GAF ratings and still qualify for 100% disability!

Another reason we also go to sanctuary or remove ourselves from society is based upon another belief we had. It was a belief or feeling we all carried but didn't discuss. In our situation we knew we would never be taken as a prisoner of war because of who we were (we were a prize catch) and the bounty we carried on us; nor would we take prisoners. The last man standing was the winner. Being in society where you do not trust anyone, and because you are always on defense, is in essence like being in a war. Everyone you pass on the street is a potential enemy. If, and I say "if" very, very carefully, our defensive boundaries or limits were overstepped and we were threatened, then we wouldn't take any prisoners or be taken prisoner. It would be the last man standing is the winner. Why is that? They forgot to install an off switch! And remember rule number 1, that I talked about earlier in the book: we have no rules. We know it would be a very ugly situation if a scenario of this type took place. By removing ourselves from society, limiting our exposure to people or crowds, and going to sanctuary, we have greatly reduced the chances of confrontation. That is part of the price we are paying. Any figures yet?

Too many people glorify war and think 'Nam wasn't so difficult or we didn't have it so rough. Now, I am very good with math but I cannot come up with an equation to calculate the price I paid for serving my Country, can you? If you want, ask Gary what price he paid for serving his country and see what his answer is. Remember, he has a bad back from his crash on Co Pung. Heart disease that is related to Agent Orange, bad knees, pancreas problems plus numerous other health problems, two divorces, P.T.S.D. (100% disability), needs sanctuary, sleeps with one eye open, flashbacks and nightmares, dislikes being around people, and many other things. I am sure he would tell you that he paid a very heavy price.

Another person to ask about paying the price is my friend and neighbor, Hughie. He still carries a fragment on the top of his skull, has migraine headaches, sleeps with one eye open, Agent Orange problems, P.T.S.D. (100% disability), divorced once, flashbacks, and the nightmares about Timmy. Hughie is the individual referred to in the "Saving Pvt. Ryan" chapter. He retrieved Timmy's upper torso so both halves could be buried together. Do you think he has paid the price?

And how about my friend Howard "Pappy" Grabill? His Parkinson's has gotten worse. He has undergone brain surgery to hopefully help control the tremors, and needs back surgery in the near future. Parkinson's is quietly being linked by the V.A. to Agent Orange. He also has P.T.S.D., back problems, been divorced once and other problems from 'Nam. Has he paid the price?

And how about Don "Wild Bill" Corey? He struggled through 3 painful years with an enlarged prostate that the doctors could only blame on Agent Orange. After much treatment, they were finally able to reduce the size of the prostate gland, but the medicine was so strong that it damaged the liver. Don has been a recluse for over 10 years now and has removed himself from society.

Other problems include P.T.S.D., back problems, sleeping with one eye open, divorced once and other problems from 'Nam. Has he paid the price?

And I cannot forget about Hector "Marty" Martinez. He sleeps with one eye open, has P.T.S.D., back problems, knee problems and goes to his basement for sanctuary.

I also cannot forget Billy Campbell. Billy lost his legs on Co Pung. With the help of the V.A., I found Billy was indeed alive. I did not go into depth about the effects of 'Nam with him, as he did not remember me, or any of the others, except "Marty". He must carry many problems from losing his legs and the horrible memories during his short duration on Co Pung. I do know he fired all his ammunition for his "pig" after he had lost his legs.

And only God knows the other problems we will have over time.

Except for Hector, do you notice a common denominator of divorce with four of us? By the way, Hector is the only one of us that missed Co Pung. A marriage is a union of body and spirit. It is hard to have a union when the spirit is gone or so deeply buried under the hardcore shell that we carry. To have a good marriage, it is necessary to be able to talk to your spouse and explain the problems. That is kind of hard to do when we barely understand our problems, or much less admit to them. I only feel truly comfortable in talking about my 'Nam experiences with Gary, Howard, Don, and Hector. Otherwise, people really don't understand or fathom the effect of what we went through. I was talking to Gary one day about the problems of the marriages we had been in, and the only way I could explain it was; I had twenty-five years in two marriages but I have been by myself since I left 'Nam. His answer was, I know how you feel, I am the same way. More could be said on that but I believe that the comments throughout this book answer why we are all divorced.

But we are not the only ones paying the toll. How about our children, or stepchildren, who live, or lived, with a dysfunctional father? Or how about the rest of the relatives who can't understand why you don't talk to them, or why you shy away from family events because they involve crowds. How about the wives, being afraid to climb into bed wrong, or wake up her spouse wrong. Maybe wanting to be closer to their spouse, but he is unable to show the emotion.

There are so many situations relating to our time in 'Nam because _we changed forever into someone we often times don't understand, don't like, or can't control_.

We have paid the price and we still are paying for it daily.

Would you be willing to pay the price? I doubt it!

A REUNION OF A DIFFERENT SORT

I received a letter on a Recon reunion, and to make a long story short, was given the phone number for our former Battalion, and later Brigade Commander, which is why this chapter is titled as such. All previous reunions were with the men I served with, but this was a ranking officer who knew all about Recon. This chapter was written approximately two to three years after I completed the original book. I believe it is more than appropriate to add this chapter, as it verifies many comments about Recon from a man we all had a lot of respect for.

Earlier in the book, I mentioned a Lt. Colonel who went by the nickname of "Shamrock". Much to my surprise, he lives less than seven hours from me, so needless to say, I called him to see if we could meet. I figured it was a once in a lifetime chance and maybe it would clear up some questions I had. Being as we are not getting any younger and "Shamrock" is about 76 years of age, I didn't want to waste much time for the opportunity to meet with him, if he was interested.

When I called him, his wife answered the phone and I had to explain that I was not a telemarketer, but had served under her husband in 'Nam. When he answered the phone I explained who I was, and I recanted a situation not mentioned in this book. Late in 1970, my PRC-77 radio quit on me and I needed a replacement, and there wasn't a chopper available to bring one out to us. A voice came across the PRC-25 I was using, and the individual, who identified himself as "Shamrock", was inbound with my radio. At that time he was the Brigade Commander, but had been our Battalion Commander a few weeks earlier. He immediately remembered the event and described details that I had not mentioned yet including the timeframe and approximate area of the event. In the discussion I told him my nickname of "Lambchops", that I used in the clear on the radio, and he responded with "I remember you!" I was impressed, as those events were about 33 ½ years ago. Needless to say, we planned to meet about 10 days later, for lunch.

The rest that followed was very interesting to say the least. The comments here are not necessarily in order, but placed in a sequence to give a little more flow and sense to our conversation. Hopefully, nothing is misquoted or misstated. This was not a conversation between a retired Colonel and a former Sergeant, but two old warriors with stories to tell.

"Shamrock" and the Author reuniting after 33 plus years.

I should also interject here that in 'Nam, I knew little of him, but what I did know was he was very well respected. After we had our long lunch, that lasted over 2 ½ hours, I had a tremendous amount of respect for him. I would rather follow the "Shamrock" of today into battle than most leaders I have met. He may be an old soldier but he is a very sharp, intelligent, and experienced warrior. I think his comment was something to the effect that he was the infantryman's leader, not one to sit at the Pentagon. As a matter of fact, "Shamrock" stated that he refused to be assigned to the Pentagon.

My initial thought on how to break the ice, was to apologize to him for lying on the radio so often about our position. If you remember earlier in the book, I discussed how we gave our location falsely, or called in when under mortar fire and claimed we had moved, when in reality we hadn't. This was done in order to get artillery called in closer than allowed and much closer than "danger close". In our conversations about 'Nam I told him about lying to him on the radio, and he laughed it off, commenting that we hadn't fooled him a bit. You may have fooled everyone else he replied, but I knew what you were doing and why you were doing it. Now that comment may not sound like much to the average person, but you have to remember, he was a career man. For a career Lt. Colonel to knowingly allow his troops to break rules, and break them big time, was putting his career on the line. His future would have looked bleak if Recon had had injuries or lost men to "friendly fire" because of a mistake that he knowingly allowed to happen. It shows that he had a lot of confidence in Recon and the experience that we had. Maybe he used the same rulebook that we used. Remember rule number 1? We had no rules!

Speaking of the radio "games" we played; I told "Shamrock" of the story told earlier in the book about "Wild Bill" and I pretending to be Line Company R.T.O.'s. As I told the story to him, you could see his eyes light up as he was enjoying our antics and the resulting outcome. The smile on his face and the look in his eyes made telling the story more than worthwhile.

I think the thing that impressed me the most was his respect for Recon. He referred to Recon as the best unit in the 101st and quite possibly the Army. No matter how you look at it, that is quite a compliment from a man of his experience and caliber, and in that respect, it is quite a compliment to receive from anyone! Many chapters back I stated that Recon was rated the #1 platoon in the 101st for two years running, and "Shamrock" verified the statement again.

I felt it my duty and responsibility to explain to him how being in 'Nam and Recon had affected all of us (more on this later). I also wanted to know how it affected him and his attitude towards casualties.

I mentioned in an earlier chapter about Recon having front row seats for the Bob Hope Christmas show. I asked him how Recon received the cherished seating.

"Shamrock" explained that apparently it came about as a result of Major General Hennessy (the Commanding General of the 101st), wanting him to bring in the whole battalion for the show. "Shamrock's" reply was "no sir"! And his explanation was, we have taken too much ground and if we sustain even one casualty in retaking the ground, it is not worth seeing the show! But if anyone deserves the front row seats it is Recon, they are the best!

First of all, it reinforces his opinion of Recon and how good we were. But I was thoroughly impressed with his reasoning. You often hear of officers figuring that they are doing good if they have a low casualty rate or if their rate of casualties is lower than expected. Not with "Shamrock". If he had one casualty, it was one too many. I cannot think of anything more impressive in describing a commanding officer's attitude towards his troops. This doesn't mean he didn't make mistakes, but it tells me that he really cared for his troops. His track record in 'Nam apparently reflected his philosophy. He stated that during his tenure in 'Nam, the O'Deuce had the lowest casualty rate in the 101st Airborne Division. Actions do speak louder than words.

In the very beginning of the book, I referred to Recon as an elite unit.

Very surprisingly, in our discussions about how good Recon was, he said Recon was an <u>elite</u> unit. If you look in a dictionary for the definition of elite, it will tell you "it is the cream of the crop, the best". I think it is no coincidence that both of us referred to Recon as an "elite" unit. As this chapter goes on, I think the reason I say this will become obvious.

As we discussed Recon and the difficulties we had, he brought up the five levels of hardship that he uses in speeches and was a topic he discussed with new troops in the O'Deuce. I personally did not hear the speech from him, as I was in the rear only a few hours before joining Recon in the bush. He mentioned that he is often asked to speak about soldiers' hardships. One of his opening questions is "how many of you have carried a weapon in combat?" This is to give him a sense of what his audience understands about war fighters. He then explains the five levels of hardship to them. The first level of hardship in combat is being cold. But it gets worse.

"Cold and wet," I replied. "I've been there."

"You're right," he said. "But it gets worse than that. Cold, wet, and hungry is level three."

All I could do was nod my head and quietly said, "Yep, been there too."

"Cold, wet, hungry, and tired is level four," he went on.

"And being shot at makes it worse," I commented without thinking. "Been there too!"

"You are right again," he responded. <u>"And Recon had it the worst!"</u>

Again, I think that says a lot when you consider his background and experience. When you place his comments of five levels of hardship, in perspective with his experience with other troops he has led through the years, his background of commanding jungle school training, and knowledge from other commands through his career, and he proclaims that Recon had it the worst, it is not a mild statement in any form. Considering everything, it is a very strong statement that helps to explain why we are so messed up from our time in 'Nam and Recon.

No disrespect to "Shamrock's" five levels of hardship, but there are six levels of hardship. To fully understand level six, you must remember all the horrors and pain from the chapter titled "The Rucksack and The Hump". Level six is humping a 100 to 120-pound rucksack in the monsoons, being cold, wet, hungry, tired and being shot at.

I mentioned earlier that part of my obligation to my Recon brothers was to tell and explain how difficult 'Nam was on us. While the five levels of hardship touch on the subject, it only skims the surface in many areas, not explaining the problems we carry after 'Nam. At some point I intend for "Shamrock" to have an opportunity to read this book, but being as he hadn't at the time of our meeting, I had a lot of explaining to do. I had to explain that being cold and wet is only partially accurate. During the 'soons being cold and wet takes on a new meaning. Especially when you only have three showers in 5 months. I needed to explain, as we ate in the restaurant, why I was watching everyone go by and being defensive all the time. Why I still sleep with "one eye open" and have nightmares. The stomach problems all of us have from drinking the bad water. Physical problems from carrying the heavy Ruck through the jungles and on combat assaults. The lingering effects of being hardcore. Just look in the eyes; the eyes tell it all! Obviously, everything was not explained in a short paragraph, as here, but as with many conversations, we bounced back and forth between subjects as we were enjoying our time together.

I brought up the subject of the assault on Co Pung Mountain, which was after his tour in 'Nam (he left 'Nam in February of 1971) and the effects it had on us, including the two to three week timeframe after which none of us can remember anything. Also, being unable to remember being made the Platoon Leader and several weeks later, being relieved of my position and kicked out of the field.

"Shamrock's" replacement as Battalion Commander didn't have a clue about commanding a combat unit. Lt. Colonel "X" was too long on staff time and too short on combat experience. His lack of appropriate actions on Co Pung and afterwards was quite obvious. He didn't know the difference between his helmet and a hole in the ground (I'm being polite here). Lt. Colonel "X" relieved me of my position and kicked me out of the field because I would not turn on my strobe light in the middle of the night when my short-handed Recon team was surrounded by major elements of a North Vietnamese battalion. Lt. Colonel "X" jeopardized our lives by circling our position and pinpointing our location. I made the right decision that night, and we all knew it. But it was nice to have it reaffirmed 33 years later by an old soldier that does know his helmet from a hole in the ground.

"Shamrock" also explained how he always had the next one or two Platoon Leaders picked out before one was needed. To keep his Captains that were in charge of Line Companies on their toes, he would often place a First Lieutenant in charge of a company. Which is exactly what happened with Lt. Bridges, mentioned earlier in the book, when he left Recon.

Somewhere in the conversations concerning the effects of 'Nam on me, he popped the question "did I go to a duty station stateside after 'Nam to "readjust" or to "come down". This was because he had concerns during his tours of 'Nam (he had three) about the after effects. I believe this goes back to his concern for his troops. "Shamrock", a devout catholic, was truly concerned for the welfare of his men. I explained that, after being kicked out of the field, I went into the division TOC for about 10 weeks, and then home. For many combat troops, 2 or 3 months stateside would have helped. The degree to which it would have helped would have depended on what they had been through and other personal factors. For those of us in Recon, it probably would have been irrelevant. Being as the effects were buried deep inside. Denial, hardcore, and everything mentioned throughout this book have made the effects irreversible.

One thing that needs to be added here is a topic we did not discuss but fits appropriately. A huge majority of Recon men use some form or combination of their past unit, or numbers relating to places, or their time in 'Nam for e-mail addresses, password numbers, computer names, etc. Part of "Shamrock's" e-mail address is 2/502. Do you think this is an indicator that commanding the O'Deuce had an influence on him?

After a couple of hours of wonderful conversation with my former Battalion Commander, I had one more question for him. Again, the information is placed in an order to follow a train of thought and is not a word for word recital. I started out with, "Sir, we have had some excellent conversations and comments about Recon and 'Nam. But I have one question for you that you might shed some light on for me. Who were we?" The question left a surprised look on his face, so to help with the answer I started off. "Sir, let me start off with the reasons I ask this question; because I am not trying to blind-side you because of the respect we have for each other. First of all, is my record from 'Nam. The V.A. explicitly stated that my records were not available. The law firm handling my case could not find any information on me. And remember, they dig long and hard because helping vets is their only source of income."

He thought for a moment and said, "The records are there; they just didn't look hard enough. Besides, you were on somebody's morning report!" He thought for a brief moment and said that possibly the records could have been destroyed or buried very deeply. Having a Recon unit wiped out would have been very damaging to anyone's career. Destroying or hiding the records, or making them difficult to see would explain the inability to find them. This showed me just how sharp "Shamrock" still is. The answer was wrong though, and I proceeded on with more information. I also thought to myself that Lt. Colonel "X" didn't have the brains to come up with such a concept. Also notice that "Shamrock" stated we were on someone's morning report, which is a correct and accurate statement, but he didn't say whose.

I continued on, "Sir, you need to understand that the V.A. didn't say they were lost but unavailable for viewing. They are still classified. I was told by the V.A. that Recon was a black unit and only one person in the V.A. system has a high enough security clearance to view my records."

I also explained that Social Security showed I had only one year of military service until my V.A. disability came through. And how about the choppers we flew on? Most of the time they were unmarked. I also explained several other details I have encountered and mentioned throughout the book.

His response to the details was an excellent summation of alternative possibilities and attempting to explain the questions, with answers that simply worked around the answer, or very discretely changed the subject.

This was the type of answer I expected, but one thing hit me as I was digesting his comments. He never once flatly denied my answer with a "no". Knowing that I did not want to ruin a perfectly great reunion by pushing too much, I decided to drop the question, except for one detail.

"Okay," I said. "But sir, could you explain this for me?" And at that point I pulled out an affidavit for him to read. The affidavit was heavily blacked out. It was a copy of the affidavit mentioned in the previous chapter. The affidavit openly states that Recon 2/502 was a black operations unit, under the control of the CIA and other groups, in fact a SOG unit. The affidavit has more information than that, but in order to maintain the proper respect for the author, it is appropriate not to mention any more. You will also notice that, throughout this chapter I have mentioned my former Battalion Commander by "Shamrock" only. I have not mentioned him by name, the town we met in, or where he lives out of the same respect. It is necessary to give enough information to maintain the credibility of the details in this book but no more needs to be disclosed.

He read over the affidavit slowly, and he had a perplexed look on his face as he read it. I assumed the look was because he didn't expect me to have hard evidence on the question. After reading the affidavit his first question was of no surprise.

"Where did this come from?" he asked.

"Sir, you know I cannot answer that, but it is genuine. The individual's security clearance is as high or most likely higher than yours. And that is all I can say."

He tried to dilute the strength of the affidavit by saying the individual may have had a high security clearance, but it was compartmentalized. Meaning a high clearance but in a very narrow scope.

"No," I responded. "But the only other thing I can say is this individual used to work with the people that had set up Recon as a black unit."

He pondered for a moment and asked me if it helped me get my disability.

"Yes," I answered.

"Good," he replied.

End of subject.

I knew when to stop and this was the best place to stop. "Shamrock" confirmed in some way what I knew. Not by what he said, but by what he didn't say. He never denied Recon was a black unit. He never said "no"! He offered excellent alternative possibilities and very slyly evaded answers by asking questions or changing the subject back and forth in an effort not to answer. One and one equals two, and the alternatives didn't add up correctly.

There were a couple of other comments that he made to give "hints", and because of his code of silence, he could not answer directly and say, "this is who you really were".

For example, during our discussions, I mentioned that I do not watch television anymore so I don't have the foggiest clue to what is going on in the world; and I don't, nor do I care. Sometime shortly thereafter we were discussing Recon then and now; or what "now" would be like for Recon.

Recon as we knew it would be a small, hard-hitting Task Force today.

As I mentioned, I don't have a clue to what is going on in the world. So I asked "Shamrock" what type of comment could I place here so people of today could make a comparison of the Recon of old verses Recon of new. His answer was simple. "You can't. People of today do not know anything about your Task Force."

While the rest of the 101st is back at Fort Campbell, Kentucky, there are still troops in Afghanistan; their mission is to find Osama Bin-laden. Sounds like strong, well-armed proud men are still carrying on the tradition. Just like Recon 2/502 of old.

That comment, "people of today do not know anything about your task force", was another hint about us I believe, because he could not say anymore.

When I took him home, we talked some more and he mentioned that he wanted to read my book. I responded that I would be happy for him to read and review my book but I only had one issue to reconcile; my affidavit.

We then shook hands and I hit the road. I started processing all that was said and realized that he answered who we were.

And ultimately, it is absolutely, positively irrelevant whether we were or were not a black or clandestine unit. It is irrelevant in the final outcome if Co Pung was or was not an attempt to have us eliminated. All of that is meaningless in the final analysis. All the debating, questions or gray areas regarding us is absolutely irrelevant and meaningless. In the end, it does not change one shot fired, nor does it change one second we spent in the jungle, nor does it change one incoming round, nor does it change one combat assault; it doesn't bring back Billy's legs, it doesn't change a single, solitary thing. And I cannot over-emphasize this enough! One, and only one fact, is important here. It is the clear, unavoidable and undeniable truth. We were Recon 2/502 of the 101st Airborne Division. The best of the best. The final outcome of what we went through and the effects it had on us does not change because of whom we worked for. We went to Hell and back; and those that survived are still paying the price today. These facts are absolute. This was the primary reason for this book: to tell what we went through and how it has affected us. Who we did it for, in the end, is very meaningful and relevant. It is best stated by saying we did it for our Country: The United States of America.

With all that being said, you ask yourself why the effort to prove Recon was a black unit? It is simple. Envision a very large picture hanging on the wall of a room with an impressive frame around it. The picture shows all the men that served in Recon, both living and deceased. It would be a great picture to see. America's best! As you look around the room you realize the picture would be better served if it were moved slightly and placed in better light. This is my reasoning exactly. Recon was a great unit but we should be looked at in a better light.

A final comment. "Shamrock" quoted an old saying during our lunch, "There are no atheists in foxholes". After rereading this book and after long discussions with "Pappy", "Wild Bill", "Four Eyes", and "Marty", we know that GOD exists, because if HE didn't, we would have breathed our last breath in 1971. "GOD bless America"!

Post comment:

I met with "Shamrock" after he had the opportunity to read this book. His comments about this book are on the back cover. A few minor corrections in this chapter were suggested and made. As the topic of Recon being a black or clandestine unit is a sensitive or gray area, I thought I would give him the final choice or opportunity to end the question or debate by removing it from this book. So I asked him a simple question before I left. Should I take it out of the book? His answer: I wouldn't take it out! End of subject!

IN CLOSING

The purpose of this book is to be a history lesson for our children and an educational tool for the average American that was never in combat. Even though the events in this book are about the unit I was in or parts of my personal life, it is simply a matter of changing the name of the writer, the unit, the major battle or firefight, and possibly a wound or two. Change a few personal details and this book becomes the personal story for tens of thousands of other 'Nam vets, regardless if they were Army or Marines.

If you change the wording in "And Paying The Price", it applies to just about any combat soldier. Whether they fought in WW2, Korea, Vietnam or in the conflicts of today, the results of "Serving Our Country and Paying The Price" are real. You may or may not agree with my comments and beliefs, but that is your choice. But the price of freedom isn't free. And if it wasn't for the combat veteran, you would not be living in a country where you could disagree, state your opinion or have your choice.

My hope is that this book has helped in some way either the vet or his friends and family recognize that his life in the bush or in a conflict wasn't easy and he needs understanding; not sympathy.

For the vets that served their country and especially those that carried rifles in the bush; my "boonie" cap is off to you! This book is about you.

I hope this has given you some insight and understanding of things we experienced and why we act and react the way we do. And why we will never be "normal".

Remember why we are hardcore.

Remember what the eyes are telling you when you look into our eyes.

Remember that we used to be different.

Remember that we did not ask to change.

Remember our close calls.

And remember..........not all of us made it back!

Richard "Lambchops" Price
"Strike Force 2/502"

DEFINITIONS

11B: A military M.O.S. indicating an infantry back round.

11F: A military M.O.S. indicating a background in operations and intelligence.

A.I.T.: Advanced Individual Training

Advanced Individual Training: A training program lasting about 10 to 12 weeks to further troops in their field of specialty, also known as M.O.S.

Agent Orange: A defoliant sprayed over the jungle in an effort to clear the vegetation and overgrowth. It was later classified as a dioxin.

AK-47: The weapon most commonly used by the North Vietnamese.

A.P.C.: Armored Personnel Carriers.

Arc Lights: B-52 bombers dropping their bombs.

Artillery: Cannons that vary in size and fire explosive projectiles that vary in diameter from 105mm (a little over 4 inches), 155mm, 175mm and 8 inch.

B-52: A large U.S. bomber.

Barracks: A large open building for housing troops. All bunk beds and lockers are in the open and oriented in rows.

Basic Training: The initial 8-week training period that focuses on elementary military rules and discipline.

Bird: A Huey helicopter also referred to as a slick.

Black: A term indicating an operation or unit is classified or hidden.

Booby trap: A device to cause harm or death. There are thousands of configurations.

Boonies: The jungle or the bush.

Boonie cap: A soft fabric jungle hat that didn't make noise.

Brass: A slang term referencing officers in a command position. Can also mean empty shell casings ejected from rifles or cannons.

Bush: The jungle, also referred to the boonies or the field.

C-4: A plastic explosive used in claymore mines and to cook with when needed.

C rations: Canned food that included our source of fruits and canned meats.

C.A.'s: Combat assaults.

Cammys: Camouflaged jungle fatigues

Charlie: The Viet Cong or Charlie Cong

Charlie rats: "C" rations.

Chopper: Helicopter, slick or bird.

Claymore mine: An explosive device that expels steel balls upon activation. The mine is placed on the ground on short legs and aimed for a waist high engagement. It contains approximately 1 pound of C-4 explosive.

Clear: Or "in the clear" indicated talking on the radio without coding of location or names.

Click: 1000 meters, 1.6 clicks equal a mile. Also listed as a "k" (kilometer).

Cobra: A helicopter gunship. Thinner than the Huey and carries 7.62mm mini guns, 40 mm grenade launcher, rockets mounted on the sides or occasionally 20mm cannon. Armament varies from helicopter to helicopter.

Combat Assaults: Using helicopters and gun ships to insert and extract troops.

Company: A unit in a military battalion. Approximately 100 people made up of three or four platoons.

Daisy cutter: A large parachute guided bomb designed for an airburst. It weighs approximately 10,000 pounds.

Danger close: A term indicating a minimum safe proximity to an explosion or artillery.

Delta 1: A radio device that was attached to the PRC77 for scrambling and decoding transmissions.

Dioxin: A chemical compound that causes cancers and many other health problems.

DMZ: Demilitarized Zone-The section of land that divided North and South Vietnam.

Doggies: A Marine slang for the grunts in the field.

D ring: A "D" shaped snap ring that attached to a Swiss seat for rappelling.

E-tool: An entrenching tool used to dig foxholes with. Has a folding handle and is similar to a shovel.

Fast flyers: Any type of jet fighter in a support role.

Firebase: Artillery or mortars oriented in a pattern to effectively fire in support of troops.

Firefight: An exchange of gunfire between two sides in an effort to eliminate the others.

Flashback: A situation in which you may be awake or asleep and a trigger mentally overtakes you and you are reliving a combat situation or condition.

Freefire: A condition that allows you to shoot at anyone at any time.

Gooks: Slang for Orientals

Grunts: The infantryman in the Line Companies or the field.

Hardcore: A state of mind; see the chapter for complete explanation.

Heat tab: A foil wrapped blue heating tablet used for cooking and keeping warm with.

Hooch: Typically two ponchos tied or snapped together and placed approximately   waist high.

Hump: Carrying the rucksack in the jungle.

Humping: See hump.

Humpers: The person carrying the ruck and is humping.

In Country: A term implicating you are in the country of Viet Nam.

Infantry: Typically the riflemen in the field with an 11B M.O.S.

Jar heads: An Army slang term for Marines.

K.I.A.: Killed in action.

Leeches: A blood-sucking parasite found commonly in swamps or wet areas.

L.R.R.P.: Long Range Reconnaissance Patrol. Sometimes platoon is used in place of patrol.

L.R.R.P. rations: Our main source of food. These were freeze-dried and all was needed was water.

L.Z.: Helicopter landing zone. Also listed as a lima zulu.

M-16: A rifle capable of semi automatic or automatic fire. 5.56mm (.223) caliber. This weapon was the standard issue rifle.

M-60: A 7.62 (.308) caliber machinegun. Also referred to as "the pig"

M-79: A 40-mm grenade launcher, similar to a short single shot shotgun.

Meter: A meter is a metric unit of measurement that is 39.37 inches.

Monsoons: The relentless rainy season. Also referred to as the 'soons.

Mortar: A high angle projectile fired from a ground orientated tube. Used by both the U.S. and Vietnamese.

M.O.S.: Military Occupational Specialty or your career field in the service; i.e. a cook or infantryman.

'Nam: An abbreviation of Vietnam.

N.C.O.: Non Commissioned Officer. Typically referred to as a Sergeant.

N.C.O. school: A twelve-week course to train individuals to lead.

N.D.P.: Night defensive position; a place that you believe to be a defendable spot and set up for the night.

Newby: A new person in country or your unit. In other books referred to as "FNG".

N.V.A: The North Vietnamese Army.

O'Deuce: Indicates the 2/502 or the 02 portion.

O.J.T.: On the job training.

Olive drab: The green color adopted by the military for uniforms and accessories

PRC-25: The standard radio used for communications. Weighed approximately 25 lbs.

PRC-77: Very similar to the PRC25 except the electronics allowed it to be used with a "Delta 1" for secure transmissions.

Pig: An M-60 machine gun.

Radioman: Carried a radio to communicate with. Typically a PRC-25 or 77.

Platoon: A military unit of 20 to 30 men typically. Three or four platoons create a company.

Poncho: A piece of rain gear that is rectangular in shape with a place for the head to go through.

Poncho liner: A lightweight quilted insert for a poncho but primarily used as a cover or blanket.

Pop Smoke: Pulling the pin on a smoke grenade and indicating your position.

Rappelling: The act of a controlled slide down a 100-foot rope with a Swiss seat, d ring and gloves.

Recon: Simply stated as searching an area. Also referred to as reconnaissance.

Resupply: Helicopters bringing in food, clothing, and other necessities.

Red team: Two cobras working in tandem.

R.E.M.F.: Rear echelon blankety blank.

Rock-n-roll: A term indicating you have your thumb on the weapons safety and ready to go to full automatic fire.

R.P.G.: A rocket-propelled grenade. This weapon is shoulder held and the grenade is launched from the end of the tube. Was used by the Vietnamese.

R.T.O.: A radioman; initials stand for RadioTelephone Operator. Some definitions refer to as RadioTelegraph Operator.

Ruck: A rucksack or large backpack.

Rucksack: The pack carried that contained all your food and necessary equipment.

Sapper: A N.V.A. that is very well trained in crawling and carries an explosive device and a handgun.

Shake-n-bake: A term referred to graduates of N.C.O. School because of the relatively short time involved in obtaining rank.

Slick: A Huey helicopter; also referred to as a bird.

Snake: A cobra gunship.

S.O.I: Standard operating index also referred to as the "magic wheel". This device allowed you to code and decode information.

Standdown: The unit coming out of the field for a few days of rest.

Stars and Stripes: A military published newspaper distributed to troops.

Swiss seat: A simple rope seat created to make a semi comfortable harness for rappelling.

Thumper: AN M-79 grenade launcher.

T.O.C.: Tactical operations center: The command center for a unit, regardless of Battalion or Division level.

V.C.: The people of a village that were the barbers, etc during the day and the enemy at night. (Viet Cong).

White Power round: (W.P.) White phosphorus artillery round. Also referred to as a Willy Pete or a Wilson Picket round

X.O.: Executive officer or second in command.

READER'S COMMENTS

The author is a man I fought side by side with in the jungles of Vietnam. We went there as teenagers and returned home as men, as survivors. In this book he looks into the soul of the Recon soldier.

Don "Wild Bill" Corey
Recon 2/502

Learn what it is to be hardcore, the state of mind and body of a combat grunt, and how a rational being deals with the rest of his life. Better than any ivory tower study.

I would highly recommend this book to anyone that really wants to know the price one pays being a warrior for democracy and freedom.

James P. Brinker; Recon 2/502, Vietnam 1970: author "West of Hue; Down the Yellow Brick Road."